DISCARD

Library Media Skills
and the
Senior High School English Program

TEACHING LIBRARY MEDIA RESEARCH AND
INFORMATION SKILLS SERIES

Edited by Paula Kay Montgomery

Library Media Skills and the Senior High School English Program.
By Mary H. Hackman.

Library Media Skills: Strategies for Instructing Primary Students.
By Alice R. Seaver.

**Media Skills for Middle Schools: Strategies for Library Media
Specialists and Teachers.** By Lucille W. Van Vliet.

Ready for Reference: Media Skills for Intermediate Students.
By Barbara Bradley Zlotnick.

LIBRARY MEDIA SKILLS

and the
Senior High School English Program

MARY H. HACKMAN

EDITED BY
PAULA KAY MONTGOMERY

1985
Libraries Unlimited, Inc.
Littleton, Colorado

LIBRARIES UNLIMITED, INC.
P.O. Box 263
Littleton, Colorado 80160-0263

Library of Congress Cataloging in Publication Data

Hackman, Mary H., 1931-
    Library media skills and the senior high school
English program.

    (Teaching library media research and information
skills series)
    Includes index.
    1. High school students--Library orientation.
2. School libraries (High school) 3. Instructional
materials centers. 4. Media programs (Education)
5. English language--Study and teaching (Secondary)
I. Montgomery, Paula Kay. II. Title. III. Series.
Z675.S3H22 1985 025.5'678223 84-28895
ISBN 0-87287-419-2

This book is dedicated to my students.

They have taught me far more than I could ever teach them.

Special thanks to my family.

Table of Contents

Foreword

Library media skills instruction for the senior high school student must involve both an opportunity for complete mastery of any basic skills that may have been missed and a refinement of those skills so that more intense study and mental growth can be achieved. In· the student's work in the library media center, there must also be time to study content areas. This work will require both basic research skills, which students should soon master, and the more subtle skills of study and information retrieval. In the high school years, it becomes increasingly difficult to pull the library media center out of the subject areas, since the resources of the center contribute more to the course content than ever before.

If the senior high school library media specialist is aware of the courses taught and is an active member of the teaching staff in the school, there will be more than enough opportunities to integrate library media skills instruction with various subject areas. A primary place is, of course, the English/Language Arts program, not only for the study of literature but also for learning how to produce information for others through writing reports and research papers. The study skills processes taught in the high school English program are the basis for use of library resources for the rest of the student's life. The library media specialist and the high school English teacher have much in common. They are working on similar instructional goals and objectives. Here is an opportunity for the library media specialist to make the holdings of the library media center more useful to students and for the teacher to expand the thinking of students.

The author has focused on the role of both the library media specialist and the English teacher in making the relationship of library media skills and English instruction a viable one. Discussions of how to publicize all services and how to create an environment where give and take occur are carefully presented through actual examples. Suggestions for interaction and units of study are provided as models. All the ideas in this book have actually been tried and have worked with great success.

The author, Mary Hackman, has been a library media specialist at the high school level in Anne Arundel County Public Schools, Maryland. She is now the library media administrator, or supervisor, for library and media services in Baltimore County Public Schools. In both roles, she has had the opportunity to assist teachers and other educators and to help improve library media programs. She has had many opportunities to serve as a resource person modeling successful practices for library media personnel.

The first chapters of this book provide a conceptual framework in which goals are discussed and roles and relationships are defined. Later chapters provide the specifics of how to put this conceptual framework into operation.

Both the author and series editor hope that the ideas presented in this document will provide a useful guide in implementing a library media skills program in the senior high school English program.

Paula Kay Montgomery

Preface

Library Media Skills and the Senior High School English Program demonstrates ways in which library media personnel and senior high school English personnel can work together to integrate instruction. Actual examples for integrated instruction are used and the reader is encouraged to adapt these examples for his or her own use at the district level and at the school level. Credit for the examples used in this book goes to library media and English personnel in the state of Maryland. Each model cited in this book has been observed by the writer, and while it is certain that there are many other exemplary programs in Maryland, as well as in the other 49 states, special acknowledgment must go to:

Anne Arundel County Public Schools

A. Brian Helm, Director, Library Media Services

Sally Cuttler, Jill Gann, Don Gobbi, Vera Holt, Jane Love, Mona Mandley, and Bonnie Thompson for *Scope and Sequence of Library Media Skills.* Very special thanks to Cindy Krimmelbein whose lesson on special reference books at the middle school level was adapted by Bonnie Thompson for use with an advanced composition class.

Baltimore County Public Schools

Mary Ellen Saterlie, Associate Superintendent, Division of Instruction

Benjamin P. Ebersole, Director of Curriculum, Emeritus

Jean Kuhlman, Coordinator, Office of English, and the many individuals who worked on the language arts curriculum for Baltimore County

Personnel from the Office of Library and Media Services.

Montgomery County Public Schools

Frances Dean, Director, Department of Instructional Resources

Linda Crump and Virginia Lucey from Gaithersburg Senior High School for sharing their lesson on *Readers' Guide to Periodical Literature*, their schedule, and the microcomputer form.

Prince George's County Public Schools

    Edward W. Barth, Supervisor, Library and Media Services

    Ann McMurtrey, Southern Area Library Media Specialist, who coordinated the efforts of Delores Douglas, Cheryl Gerring, Joyce Henderson, and Linda Sweeting to produce *Integrating the Library Media Skills Program into the Language Arts Curriculum, 7-12.* Others involved in this project were the staff of Palmer Park Services, Lebertha Gipson, Northern Area Library Media Specialist, Donald Kauffman, Supervisor of English Language Arts, Jack Cole, Supervisor of Reading, Dorothea Coss, library media specialist at Largo High School and the Middle School Team.

Very special thanks to Paula Kay Montgomery, editor, whose guidance and encouragement made this book happen and Linda Widows, secretary extraordinaire, who typed the manuscript.

RESPONSIBILITIES OF THE LIBRARY MEDIA SPECIALIST

The senior high school library media specialist has both a unique opportunity and an awesome task. Theoretically (and realistically) every student who enters high school will come into contact with the library media specialist. The vocational student, the gifted and talented, the dropout, the special education student, and the average student will come away from high school with an impression of the library media center and the people in it. As surely as every student leaves with an impression of the library media specialist, every teacher comes to the high school with an impression made from past experiences of what to expect from the library media specialist. What, then, should be expected of the library media staff in the senior high school?

The library media specialist must be knowledgeable about every course taught in the high school, familiar with every member of the faculty and the administrative staff, and a viable part of the school community as a whole. It is equally important that the school staff understand the large budgetary commitment required to operate a high school library media center. In addition to personnel, the budget provides for the inventory of quantities of print and nonprint materials, equipment to be supplied to every department, facilities for dark rooms and television production, sound studios, microcomputer laboratories, innumerable supplies, and the storage to house everything. While it might be easy to see the physical aspects of the center, there are many facets of the library media specialist's task that may not be readily apparent. The library media specialist is responsible for selecting, ordering, receiving, recording, cataloging, labeling, filing, placing, organizing, circulating, retrieving, inventorying, repairing, discarding, and replacing all the materials and equipment for which the library media center is held accountable. In addition, even the most elaborate and extensive library media center is merely a repository if the library media specialist is not an active member of the school's instructional staff. In order to integrate library media skills into the curriculum, the library media specialist must take into account all materials and equipment, all knowledge of teachers and courses, and all skills that the library media specialist brings to the process of learning. The library media specialist is a teacher with insight into the entire curriculum offered in the school. An awesome task indeed. All too often under the press of the many duties to be performed, and in spite of the good intention of teaching high school students to be lifelong independent users of libraries, the library media specialist points to the card catalog when a question is asked. If the student has no idea where to begin to search for an answer to his question, he or she will be quickly frustrated and will begin to form a negative image of the library media specialist that can be difficult to change. If, however, a library media specialist teaches the student the process for finding the answers to questions, the student may need only a few verbal reminders to lead him or her in the right direction and the student will have a positive image upon which to build. How well does the library media specialist succeed in leading students to the right answers? How much of the teaching done in the high school library media center carries over into life after high school?

EFFECTIVENESS OF TEACHING LIBRARY MEDIA SKILLS

There is damning evidence that the senior high school library media specialists are not being very effective in teaching library skills. Institutions of higher learning have added the library media specialist to the list of public school personnel who send them students who are ill prepared in basic skills. One librarian from the University of Evansville in Illinois wrote in the *School Library Journal* in 1979,

> After two years of administering a very active undergraduate program, I find that incoming freshmen—*without a single exception that I have observed* lack all but the most rudimentary library skills. Not only are they unable to use reference tools, they have no inkling of what sources are available. They don't know when to ask questions or even what to ask for; they do not know whether a librarian has served them badly or well. For them, the unbounded universe of information is, literally, a closed book.[1]

This same article stated that the incoming freshman knows how to locate information in the card catalog and can use most of the general encyclopedias. There is some evidence that the newest edition of the *Encyclopaedia Britannica* confounds him. Perhaps half of the first-year college students are able to use the *Readers' Guide to Periodical Literature* without assistance.[2] This is a serious indictment of the library media specialist working at the senior high school level, and it is all too prevalent a stance taken in the journals whose primary audience is the college or university librarian.

If the college-bound student is not getting essential library media skills in high school, it stands to reason that the other students are not getting them either. The vast majority of students will never have the opportunity to learn the necessary skills to get at that "unbounded universe of information." How can this be true? Most districts have library media skills as part of their program. Library media specialists across the nation have developed a logical scope and sequence for teaching those skills in many of our school systems. The development of a scope and sequence of library media skills gives the library media specialist a primary responsibility in the instructional program; no longer can the library media specialist function in just a supportive role.

If college librarians would take a look at scope and sequence materials for library media skills from schools across the United States, they would find that those skills with which college freshmen come equipped are usually taught in the elementary grades. The pattern for library media skills instruction in elementary school is usually one where classes are scheduled to go to the library media center for a specified period of time on a regular basis. Part of that time is used for formal instruction and practice; the remainder of the time is used for book selection. Small groups and individual students can come at any time for reference work or other kinds of library media skills related activities. Many schools prefer that the times when the elementary students come to the library media center be flexibly scheduled to allow for better integration of skills instruction into regular classroom work. The important thing is that every student in the elementary school gets library media instruction on a regular basis, whether that time is strictly scheduled or flexibly scheduled.

The library media specialist in the elementary school works with fewer teachers than the specialist at the secondary level and can accomplish more with integrated instruction, thereby making the skills taught more meaningful to the students. Since there are also fewer students at the elementary level than at the secondary level, the library media specialist can more easily address the needs of the individual child. This does not imply that the elementary library media specialist has an easy job; on the contrary, it is a demanding job that requires huge amounts of time and energy. Look at the rewards! What is taught in the elementary school library media center lasts a lifetime.

The middle school more often than not uses the example set in the elementary school—that of establishing a schedule, usually flexible, for classes to visit the library for formal and informal library media skills instruction. It is in the junior and senior high schools where this process breaks down. Although this book will examine the library media program at the senior high school level, much of what is written applies equally to the structure of the junior high school program.

What, then, are the reasons for the breakdown in the process of teaching library media skills in an integrated program at the senior high school level? In the first place, it is impossible to schedule every student in a senior high school into the library media center. Sheer numbers and lack of space and personnel make that a given. In the second place, teachers are hard-pressed to get through all of the course content they are required to cover with their classes. There are standardized tests to be administered and specified subject matter to be taught in order to meet deadlines for such tests. There are marking periods and final examinations to further harry the teacher. With the back to basics philosophy abounding in our society, as well as the push for excellence in education, the pressure on the senior high school teacher has been increased. Courses that were fun to teach and to take are being eliminated in favor of essential skills. Most teachers do not have a background in library media skills and, frankly, do not see the necessity for spending precious class time in the library media center. (It has only been in recent years that our colleges and universities have made a concerted effort to teach bibliographic skills. Library instruction is still not required by most of our institutions of higher learning—not even for those students who plan to become teachers.) The final contributing factor has to be time—or the lack thereof. The teacher usually has one planning period each day, but that does not necessarily coincide with a time that the library media specialist can meet with the teacher. The very process of sitting down to plan for integrated instruction is a time-consuming one. In reality, planning together often happens when the teacher comes to the library media center to ask when a particular class can be scheduled for the center for a specific reason. The teacher is also a member of a subject area department within the school. There are regularly scheduled department meetings in most of the senior high schools. Library media specialists who attend those department meetings find them to be fertile ground for communication and can work with the department in the process of integrating skills. However, the departments in many senior high schools always meet at the same time—faculty meetings on Monday, department meetings every other Tuesday, and so forth. The library media specialist cannot be present at all of them.

It is common practice for department chairmen to meet together on a regular schedule with members of the school administration. If the library media specialist is considered to be a department chairman, this is a golden opportunity to find out what is happening in every department and begin work toward the process of integrating instruction. The fallacy in the dependence upon these sessions is that the library media specialist is going through an intermediary (the department chairman) to get the message across to other members of the department. Department chairmen are busy people too, and there are many other matters of business to discuss besides library media skills instruction.

There is one other factor that is crucial in any discussion about high school graduates who are lacking in library media skills. Too many library media specialists—particularly at the senior high school level—do not see themselves as teachers. There are those who once were teachers and looked to the library media center as a way out of the classroom; some of these individuals readily admit that they did so to avoid the drudgery of gradebooks and correcting papers and discipline problems. They are not interested in encouraging any kind of instruction, much less pursuing the process of integrated skills instruction. Other library media specialists were graduated from colleges and universities with degrees that did not require any coursework in learning theory or teaching techniques. Library media centers operated by such individuals may well provide excellent support services to the instructional programs in the school; but to fully integrate library media skills into the curriculum, the library media specialist must accept the responsibility for teaching library media skills. Otherwise, high school graduates will continue to enter college ill-prepared to use a library.

INTEGRATING LIBRARY MEDIA SKILLS
AND SUBJECT AREA SKILLS

A bleak picture? Yes, and too often this is the reality. However, there are programs that have addressed the need for an integrated program of library media skills and all facets of the curriculum. These programs occur when there is clear direction from the library media supervisor. They occur when the supervisor and other subject area supervisors work closely and look together at goals and objectives to see how curriculum can accommodate the needs of both library media and the particular subject matter. The attitude of the supervisor permeates into the school setting and provides the climate for the library media specialist to operate more efficiently. When criteria have been clearly defined for both the classroom teacher and the library media specialist, the task of teaching library media skills is facilitated.

The term *integrated instruction* has been used often in this chapter. What is meant by integrated instruction? How does this differ from instruction that takes place in most library media centers? Thomas Walker and Paula Montgomery address these questions in their book, *Teaching Media Skills*:

> Media specialists, in the past, have sought to "relate" media skills instruction to everyday classroom teaching rather than integrate the two. Teachers, on the other hand have been perfectly willing for media specialists to "relate" media skills to classroom studies but have not, typically, *integrated* media skills objectives, activities, and assessments into instruction.
>
> The difference between the terms "relate" and "integrate" seems subtle at first, but the operational difference is enormous. *Relating* media skills to classroom instruction implies one set of instructional objectives and a separate set of media skills objectives, one set of instructional activities and a separate set of media skills activities, one set of instructional assessments and a separate set of media skills assessments, all more or less related but, at the same time, all very separate. Integrating media skills *into* classroom instruction, on the other hand, implies only one set of instructional objectives, activities, and assessments.
>
> An integrated approach to media skills instruction takes advantage of the strength and preparation of the teacher in instructional theory and methodology and the strength of the media specialist in the theory and application of instructional media. Instructional planning for media skills then emerges as a process of logically and equitably dividing labor between teacher and media specialist.[3]

Where does one begin this process of putting together instructional objectives, activities, and assessments, and drawing upon the strengths of the classroom teacher and the library media specialist? Senior high school has a multitude of courses to offer its students; some are required for graduation and others may be elected by the student for the sake of interest or vocational aptitude. The required courses that comprise the English program have a natural affinity with library media skills. In the elementary school, reading is taught by the classroom teacher and fostered by the library media specialist; the children are introduced to a wealth of children's books, films, and magazines. The elementary school child develops the habit of coming to the library media center to write reports and do projects. These kinds of activities involve aspects of the language arts or English program. At the senior high school level, every student is required to take English, usually for all four (or three) years. When the high school student is taken to the library media center for orientation in the first year of high school, it is usually with his or her freshman English class. It is in the English class where the high school student learns the processes involved in writing a research paper or doing a research project, which may well include production techniques. If one were to ask the senior high school library media specialist which department makes the most use of the materials and facilities in the center, the answer would most often be the English department. It would seem logical, then, to begin the process of integrating objectives, activities, and assessments with library media skills and the English department. There are many facets in this process and there are a variety of ways to proceed. In the following pages, we will take a look at some of the factors involved and some successful plans of action.

NOTES

[1] Mary Biggs, "Forward to Basics in Library Instruction," *School Library Journal* (May 1979):44.

[2] Ibid.

[3] H. Thomas Walker and Paula K. Montgomery, *Teaching Media Skills: An Instructional Program for Elementary and Middle School Students* (Littleton, Colo.: Libraries Unlimited, Inc. 1977), 13-14.

The English Teacher
and the Librarian

One of the facets that needs to be examined by the library media specialist or the English teacher who is considering the task of integrating library media skills instruction with the English program is a perspective of English teaching and the role of the media center and some of the rationale for change. A brief look at the last several decades can assist in this process.

BEFORE THE SIXTIES REVOLUTION

Education is no different from other fields of endeavor in that if one is around long enough, one sees the pendulum swing from one extreme to the other and back again. The English classroom is representative of such swings, despite new technologies and new approaches to learning styles and instructional methodology. Prior to the "student revolution" in the sixties, English was offered in our high schools by grade level—English 9, English 10, English 11, and English 12. Often, too, it was offered by the particular course of study pursued by the student— academic, general, or commercial. Sometimes classes were homogeneous; more often they were heterogeneous. Always class sizes were large, and English teachers counted their blessings if there were only thirty-five students in a class. Negotiated agreements were things in the distant future, and planning time was often usurped by duties, extracurricular activities, or study hall. The teacher followed a prescribed course of study for the year. If there was no course of study, the textbook and suggested activities were used. With a course of study, English was divided into units lasting from four to eight weeks encompassing composition, grammar, litera- ture, and speech. As a rule, students were required to read at least one library book each marking period and prepare a written or oral report on that book. This reading was done outside of the classroom and in addition to a variety of classics that were prescribed for each grade level. It was not uncommon for the English teacher in the fifties to have between one hundred seventy-five and two hundred students a day, and the task of grading papers was enormous. There was little time for any kind of reading guidance, and students were usually left on their own when it came to book selection.

Literature was frequently approached as a survey course and was often cor- related with the social studies program. If the tenth grade student was taking World History, then the student was also taking a world literature survey course in the

English class; if United States History was taught in the eleventh grade, a survey of American literature was the offering for the English class. While there was no real effort to make the instruction exactly parallel, there was some correlation, and the student did have the opportunity to grasp a broader view of the time about which he or she was studying.

The high school library was used as a source of books for the ubiquitous book reports and for occasional reference work. A term paper was usually a requirement in the academic twelfth grade English classes, and the library received its share of students during that endeavor. It was the exception rather than the rule for the librarian in the high school to do any formal teaching. Instead, individual students were helped to locate information for the term paper, and the broad scope of reference information was rarely introduced.

On the other hand, this writer was a high school English teacher during the fifties and does not remember ever sending English students to the high school library (much less taking them there). Instead, elaborate field trips were planned for the twelfth grade English classes to the Enoch Pratt Free Library, which was some twenty-five miles from that then relatively rural high school. At the Pratt, the students were enthralled with the architecture, awed by the pervasive spirits that inhabited the Edgar Allen Poe Room, and overwhelmed by the variety of books introduced to them by the capable librarians of that still prestigious institution. At the time, the Pratt used its own system of classification, one that was uniquely Pratt's. Undoubtedly the students were confused by the disparities between the Dewey decimal system used at school and Pratt's system. One can only hope that the students understood that libraries need to have a system for classifying materials—whatever that system might be. Many of those same students came back to the high school following their graduation to relate how they had returned from their colleges to use the Pratt's collection for research work. Considering the breadth and depth of Pratt's collection, those students were fortunate to have been introduced to one of the nation's finest public libraries. On the minus side, how unfortunate they did not have the same opportunity to appreciate the fact that their high school had a certified librarian and a small, but more than adequate collection.

THE SIXTIES

Until 1957, and the advent of Russia's Sputnik, the public had had confidence in the public school system. Egon Guba tells us that the American people then began to wonder whether the deficiencies in science and technology could not be traced to the process of education in the United States.[1] In addition to Sputnik, *Brown v. the Board of Education* in 1956 and the resulting racial integration mandated by the federal courts in 1958 placed additional demands upon our schools, affecting both our English programs and our libraries. Guba states that in the attempt to assuage the public outcry and solve the problems in the schools, educators promised too much. In turn, the public expected too much, and confidence further eroded.[2]

New Methods and Courses

The upheaval of the sixties brought about course changes in the colleges and universities. Students began to have a say in course content and structure. The senior high schools, yielding to public pressure to improve the quality of education and responding to the changes occurring in our institutions of higher learning, altered their course. Evidence quickly pointed to the fact that our schools were not adequately teaching the nation's poor or the minority groups. Educators tried instructional television, programmed learning, team teaching, and flexible scheduling—to name but a handful of the techniques tried in the sixties—but the quality of learning that ensued produced uneven results. The survey courses in American and British literature, once the bulwarks of the English curriculum and the textbook publishers, became things of the past. There were demands for the rights of the special students, for courses tailored to the needs of specific ethnic groups, and for courses that were relevant to the rapidly changing world in which we lived. English courses followed the pattern set by all subject areas, and more and more courses became semesterized at the high school level. The resulting variety of high school courses became known as "smorgasbord curriculum." Indeed, there was something for everyone; the principal problem for the student was what to take. The student coming into high school was overwhelmed by course choices, and the guidance counselor assumed the role of advisor in attempting to help sort through the myriad offerings. English classes were offered in film study, individualized reading, creative writing, theatre arts, specific literary authors, and genres. To add to the confusion, courses were given names such as Fact and Fantasy, The American Dream, and English Patterns. One had to read course descriptions carefully in order to know exactly what was being offered. Previously, Mrs. Smith and Mr. Jones had always taught eleventh grade English; now every member of the department taught semester length classes in what was often an ungraded classroom. While the number of students taught by the English teacher decreased, the number of preparations increased.

The ungraded classroom was an attempt to allow the high school student even greater freedom of choice and to take responsibility for his or her own learning. Sometimes there were prerequisites, but not always. The student could no longer assume it was correct to take World Literature in the tenth grade, because his senior sibling could be enrolled in the same course. The security of knowing that as a student you would be competing with members of your own class was gone. The more adept students were made to reach higher and harder, and the less adept were often surprised to find that they could do as well as some of the upper classmen. Of course, all students were not so fortunate.

Changes in the Library

During the sixties, school libraries were the focus of attention because they became the recipients of federal funds—part of the effort to combat the lack of student aptitude in science and technology. Senior high school collections grew; and, as monies were poured into libraries, the need for more student and teacher involvement with school libraries became apparent.

In 1969 a set of standards for librarians was written. *Standards for School Media Programs* (written as a joint effort by the American Association of School

Librarians and the National Education Association [NEA] Department of Audio-visual Instruction) used such terms as *media specialist* and *media center*. Although these standards did not advocate actually changing the titles of librarian and library, the forecast was there. The emphasis of the standards was on the vital role of the media center.[3] Things were changing; the librarian, like the rest of the educators, was going to have to run to catch up.

More interaction was now required between the librarian and the other staff members. As courses were being rewritten and as teachers were required to teach more classes, the librarian had to seek input from staff members to keep the collection up to date. It was impossible to rely on the old classics when the purpose of literature classes in the English program was to deal with the world and its current problems. There had to be interaction with the librarian if there were to be supplemental reading assignments. In many instances, the librarian became part of the teaching team and indeed was expected to teach. There were also librarians who refused to accept the fact that librarians had to add audiovisual aids and equipment to their list of holdings. Resistance to change permeated the ranks of the librarians themselves.

In 1975 a new set of standards for the school librarian was published. This time the Association for Educational Communications and Technology (formerly NEA's Department of Audiovisual Instruction) worked with the American Association of School Librarians and produced *Media Programs: District and School*.[4] While these standards were still quantitative with regard to collections and numbers of pieces of equipment, the librarian would become the library media specialist. Around the country, state departments of education would respond by changing their standards for the librarian. There was reference to program objectives, and the library media specialist emerged as a teacher. Indeed with new technologies assuming greater roles in the schools, the library media specialist was the one who was expected to change a lamp in a film projector, show the teacher how to use the video cassette recorder, and work with students to produce a slide-tape program.

THE SEVENTIES AND EIGHTIES

By the late seventies, industrial and business leaders joined the colleges and universities in telling the senior high schools that they were graduating students who were unable to do the job or pass the course because they lacked even basic skills. Colleges were spending precious time in remedial courses, and the public in general was unhappy with the state of our schools. High schools took the brunt of this criticism primarily because of declining SAT scores and the fact that high schools were supposed to prepare their students to enter the world. "Back to basics" was heard again and again in faculty rooms, college classrooms, and board-rooms. High schools began to pare away at their curriculum. Where previously it was not uncommon to offer as many as forty or fifty English courses, offerings often were cut in half. As SAT scores began to edge upward again in the early eighties, there was renewed interest in English programs. Many states across the country began to require that students pass proficiency examinations before they could graduate. Two of these examinations impacted upon the English classroom—reading and writing. The library media specialist discovered that the old classics were back in style and had difficulty convincing the publishers that it was time to reissue some of them. There is no way that education, and the English curriculum in particular, will actually go back to those pre-Sputnik days; the "world is too much with us." But, it is expected that the English teacher will work with the best from the past and continue to be adaptable to change.

In looking back at the evolving relationship of the English teacher and the librarian, it is interesting to note the many places where their roles overlap. Now, with the arrival of the microcomputer on the educational scene, the English teacher and the library media specialist continue to build that bond that has always been there. Bibliographies can now be updated with a touch of the *add* or *delete* keys. Students can sign up in the library media center to schedule a reference search via one of the many data banks that can be purchased, or they can use the word processing capabilities of the microcomputer to assist them in writing a paper. Even editing becomes a fascinating chore with the use of the microcomputer, and rewrites do not have to be tedious. An unlikely reason for bonding—reduced funding—will also keep library media specialists communicating with English teachers. Because funding is not what it was, the library media specialist must be more selective than ever when purchasing material. Among the key people who will be involved in selection will be the English teachers.

NOTES

[1] William Brickell, Speech before Maryland Library Media Specialists, Annapolis, Md., October 1975.

[2] Ibid.

[3] American Association of School Librarians and the Department of Audiovisual Instruction of the National Education Association, *Standards for School Media Programs* (Chicago: American Library Association, 1969).

[4] American Association of School Librarians and the Association for Educational Communications and Technology, *Media Programs: District and School* (Chicago: American Library Association, 1975).

This book does not pretend to provide a study on the development of curriculum design in either English or library media skills. However, this chapter will discuss some evaluation principles and some approaches to curriculum development.

EVALUATION OF PROGRAMS

Evaluative Criteria for the Evaluation of Secondary Schools, by the National Study of School Evaluation, is a document that is used to evaluate senior high school programs. Evaluation by this document and by a committee who represent it are recognized nationally as *the* evaluation tools for senior high school programs. Each school must examine the criteria and evaluate its own program prior to the arrival of the committee, which may make additional recommendations. This process of evaluation leads to accreditation of the senior high school by one of six national associations of colleges and schools. The school is judged on the basis of its own goals and objectives. The guidelines stated for the individual programs take into consideration the philosophy and goals and objectives of the particular school.

Every high school English teacher and library media specialist who has been through the evaluation process has been exposed to *Evaluative Criteria* and has had the opportunity to examine the program guidelines. *Evaluative Criteria* has guiding principles for both English and library media programs.

The fifth edition of *Evaluative Criteria* states the following principles of the English program:

> The English program is designed to improve the students' awareness of the important role that the English language and its literature play in their personal and career development. Essential to the over-all program of studies, the English program emphasizes the development of the powers of comprehension, of critical thinking skills, and of coherence, cogency, and fluency in the expression and communication of ideas.

> While the English program stresses competence in skills of reading, writing, speaking and listening, it also provides experiences and activities that will help students become discriminating users of print and

nonprint media. Literary and media works, selected for both excellence in content and style and relevance to student interests, will promote humanistic attitudes, aesthetic appreciation, and critical evaluation skills while also providing leisure time activities.*

In *Evaluative Criteria*, the library media program is called *learning media services.* The guiding principles for it are stated as follows:

One of the important purposes of the educational program is to provide the student with a variety of self-enriching ideas and experiences which lead to intellectual curiosity, achievement, and the establishment of a life-long pattern of learning.

Utilization of human resources and the full range of media which includes printed and audiovisual forms of communication and their accompanying technology are required to implement the purposes and program of the school or district.

Trends which began to receive national attention in the 1940's have influenced the development of the single administrative unit known as the media center which furnishes those services traditionally associated with the library and provides a wide variety of audiovisual and electronic services. This single administrative unit requires the skills of media professionals and nonprofessional supportive staff, e.g., para-professionals, technicians, production personnel, clerical staff, and student assistants. The media center serves not only a leadership function in improving the educational environment but also a supportive function by providing the resources for learning.**

The alignment of the two programs becomes apparent to the user of *Evaluative Criteria.* For the senior high school student to be a discriminating user of print and nonprint media, he or she must use the library media center and all of the materials housed therein. If the library media program is to instill a pattern of life-long learning, the student must have access to the human and material resources offered in the library media center.

How, then, does this happen? What can bring about a genuine integration of library media skills and a high school English program? One idea is through curriculum development. Curriculum is usually developed at the system or district level, following state guidelines and national trends.

---

*Reprinted, by permission, from National Study of School Evaluation, *Evaluative Criteria for the Evaluation of Secondary Schools,* 5th ed. (Arlington, Va.: National Study of School Evaluation, 1978), 101.

**Reprinted, by permission, from National Study of School Evaluation, *Evaluative Criteria for the Evaluation of Secondary Schools*, 5th ed. (Arlington, Va.: National Study of School Evaluation, 1978), 277.

CURRICULUM DEVELOPMENT

What, exactly, is *curriculum*? *Fundamental Curriculum Decisions*, prepared by the Association for Supervision and Curriculum Development 1983 Yearbook Committee, gives a variety of definitions for *curriculum* and *curriculum design,* but the most widely accepted definition of curriculum by educators is simply— a course of study for the learner. Curriculum as we know it today, however, reaches far beyond that "course of study" and attempts to address many other far-reaching issues. In *Fundamental Curriculum Decisions*, George Beauchamp describes curriculum as "a written plan for the educational program of a school or schools. Curriculum design then will consist of those considerations having to do with the contents, the forms and the various elements of a curriculum. We distinguish between curriculum planning and instructional planning with the curriculum planning being the antecedent task."[1] He also states "Scope and sequence have long been two major problems in curriculum design. The display of course content into topical outline is one way planners can watch for discrepancies in scope and sequence. It also helps with horizontal articulation among the various subjects."[2]

Curriculum documents usually begin with a statement of goals and objectives. (Much of the design is arbitrary and is left with the planners.) Goals are usually followed by content, content being what will actually be taught. Specific activities are included as well as a means of evaluating whether or not goals are reached. A list of possible resources is another component of most curriculum guides. One of the most important things about curriculum design is that it is never finished; it is an on-going process. When the curriculum is being revised, pieces of the original plan are often kept intact. If the curriculum is to be vital and to continue to meet the ever-changing needs in a technological society, flexibility must be the byword.

The decision to revise curriculum should never be arbitrary. Assessment of need is essential. When a district sees a need to revise its English curriculum, many factors must be considered. The decision is reached after assessing such factors as standard test scores, follow-up studies of the district's graduates, changing college requirements, and new technologies. One way to develop or revise curriculum is through the work of a carefully selected committee. The English supervisor of the district and other professional personnel form a committee to attack the revision. The committee should consist of the English supervisor, appropriate English teachers, at least one library media specialist, administrators, citizens from the community, and students. There is no set rule as to the makeup of the committee— except that it should be representative of those who will be affected by the revision.

The committee will adjust goals and objectives to meet the needs indicated in the assessment; content will be tailored to the adjusted goals and objectives; activities will be written to reflect the content; and resources will be chosen to implement the content. Methods of evaluation, an essential part of the curriculum guide, will determine how well the goals and objectives are met.

In the past, if a library media specialist was a member of the curriculum committee, his or her function was usually to determine whether or not the selected resources were in print. Sometimes that function would include seeking new materials to best suit the content and provide support for the activities as they were written. These are certainly important functions; necessary functions. How many times has curriculum been written only to discover that the resources listed were out of print and no longer available? Part of the function of every member of a curriculum committee should be to check the latest edition of *Books in Print*, current publishers' and producers' catalogs, and to acquire materials for review and evaluation prior to inclusion in a curriculum document.

The library media specialist on the committee that is responsible for revising the English curriculum should have input into the formation of the goals and objectives, the content, the activities, and the process for evaluation *as well as* the development of a current resource list. This individual should be carefully selected. He or she should be an outstanding teacher in his or her own right and should have a thorough working knowledge of the scope and sequence of library media skills. The selected individual should keep in mind that the other members of the committee come to the planning sessions with a perspective of library media specialists based upon their personal experiences with their high school library media center. If they have had negative experiences with library media specialists, they will be reluctant to turn over an important piece of their curriculum to someone about whom they do not feel very positive. The library media skills scope and sequence must be stressed; when an objective is selected for inclusion in the revised curriculum guide, the library media specialist should examine it carefully for a match with the scope and sequence of library media skills. Can library media skills be a part of the content? Can an activity be developed that will implement that content by using the library media center? How can the library media specialist assist in the assessment role of the specific objectives? What are the resources available that will most advantageously address the content and fulfill the stated objectives? These are the questions that must be answered if there is to be true alignment of library media skills and the English curriculum at the district level.

The planning/writing stage of curriculum development is merely the first step in the delivery of instruction and, ultimately, learning. Curriculum should be piloted and assessed prior to its use throughout a school or a school system. The library media staff would logically have valuable input into these important parts of curriculum development. The specialist in a school where new curriculum is being piloted may evaluate resources and determine a variety of ways in which library media services and the teacher may utilize those resources in facilitating learning. Teaching methods and learning styles may be evaluated in order to determine what works best for whom. In the experience of this writer, when library media personnel are wisely used in curriculum development, those responsible for the process seek ways to include them in future efforts.

The process of curriculum development and revision is an expensive proposition. Frequently, summer workshops provide personnel and resources to write curriculum. If curriculum is written during the school year, substitutes have to be hired to allow the teachers involved time to work together. Time and money are at a premium in school systems; obviously no district is going to rewrite curriculum every year or even every two years. Including library media personnel in the planning, the writing, the piloting, the assessing, and the revising of a program is cost-effective in determining the availability of resources. Time can be saved when the library media specialist interacts with subject area personnel during the planning and development of curriculum in order to deliver a viable library media program that meets the needs of the high school students and staff. How else can the alignment of library media skills and the English program be accomplished if the curriculum does not address the duality?

The key to success in any library media program at the school level is communication: communication with teachers, students, administrators, parents, volunteers, supervisors—every member of the school community. No matter what has or has not been written into a district or individual school curriculum guide, the library media specialist must communicate with the English department to discover what is being taught during what time period. It is important that this be done in a nonthreatening way and that it be communicated as an offer to help students broaden their knowledge through the use of the library media center. While this is an after-the-fact approach, it is the reality for many library media specialists. True alignment can occur efficiently and effectively if the library media specialist and the English teacher acknowledge the duality at the beginning of the process, rather than at the end of the process.

NOTES

[1] George Beauchamp. "Curriculum Design," *Fundamental Curriculum Decisions,* ed. Fenwick English (Alexandria, Va.: Association of Supervision and Curriculum Development 1983 Yearbook Committee, 1983), 90.

[2] Ibid., 97.

4

Relationships

In recent years, there have been a number of publications dealing with the educator and public relations. There have been articles and books that refer directly to the library media specialist in terms of public relations activities (see bibliography, pages 26-27). These publications specifically delineate procedures and practices that can be used to reach out and into the school community. The library media specialist needs to have knowledge of the techniques used in establishing good positive relations and to be able to apply them to the school situation. This chapter will deal with relationships that need to be developed with regard to the elements of the senior high school English program.

THE LIBRARY MEDIA SUPERVISOR

One of the important elements of any public relations effort is the ability to communicate effectively. Previously in this book, it has been said that the school library media specialist must have a good working relationship with every department in the senior high school; likewise, the library media supervisor must have a good relationship with every other supervisor and department at the central office level. The expression *working relationship* implies communication and the ability to work together successfully at a task. In a large school district, it is unlikely that the school-based library media personnel will have knowledge of the kinds of assistance available at the central office level other than from the library media staff. It is the responsibility of the library media supervisor (or coordinator or director) to identify those teams or individuals within a school system who can be of assistance to the school-based personnel. For example, a centrally based team working with school personnel in a program for gifted and talented students in English may provide resource help to develop library media skills activities designed for that particular clientele. Those who are responsible for implementing a microcomputer education program within the school district may provide help. The English department would be interested in understanding the word processing aspects of the microcomputer as well as management functions. What kinds of help are waiting to be tapped when the English supervisor designates a particular high school for a pilot program in mainstreaming special education students into a specific English course? It is vital that the library media supervisor know what is happening in the English program at the district level, identify sources of help for the school-based library media personnel, and communicate that information in a positive, non-threatening manner.

It behooves the library media supervisor to let supervisors in other curricular areas know the kinds of expectations they should have of the library media specialist in the schools. The English supervisor does not necessarily know that there is a scope and sequence of library media skills that can readily integrate with the English curriculum or that the library media specialist can and will teach. All too often, the specialist in the school is told by the English teacher, "I cannot bring my classes into the library media center today; I am going to be observed by my supervisor." The library media supervisor needs to communicate to the English supervisor that a library media center lesson is appropriate, meets the objectives of the curriculum, and reflects planning and assessment by the English teacher and the library media specialist.

In addition to communication with central office personnel, the library media supervisor needs to build relationships with school-based administrators with regard to the library media program. Too frequently, particularly in a large school system, the library media supervisor is called in when there is a severe problem and an image of library media personnel has already been formed that is difficult to change. Whenever possible, the library media supervisor and the English supervisor should address groups of school-based administrators together to reinforce the integration aspect of the two programs. One word of caution: supervisory personnel should not promise things that cannot be delivered. It is extremely important that the school-based library media specialist understand the goals and objectives of the system and be willing and able to carry them out prior to the supervisor's overt commitment to any plan. Principals and assistant principals are responsible for scheduling and for the ultimate success of every program within the school. They should know that there is a scope and sequence of library media skills and that the library media specialist is responsible for teaching those skills in concert with the classroom teacher. When positive relationships are built with school-based administrators, program implementation is facilitated and the library media supervisor will be invited to visit outstanding programs, as well as those that are not so outstanding.

The supervisor must know the school-based library media personnel—their abilities, their skills, their deficiencies, their needs, and their flexibility. Library media specialists should keep the supervisor informed about their goals and objectives so that the supervisor can provide the necessary help. In many senior high schools, the library media specialist is operating without the help of a fellow professional and must be able to communicate with a supervisory staff that understands the frustrations involved. In-service programs require input from the school library media specialist, and the supervisor needs to solicit that input. In-service programs can be planned jointly where library media specialists and English teachers are the intended audience. Joint planning is an efficient and valuable use of precious time. Members of the supervisory staff should let the library media specialists know when compliments about specific programs have been paid; a brief memorandum will communicate to the specialists that someone is paying attention to efforts being made.

In many school districts throughout the country, the population and area served are small enough so that the library media supervisor personally knows most members of the community. Whether the district be large or small, however, the library media supervisor should welcome opportunities to address any community group whether it be the Parent-Teacher Association or a Citizens' Advisory Council. Any positive interaction with the community on behalf of the library media program should be encouraged. Many districts seek to involve community members in the review and evaluation process in selecting library media materials or as volunteers in the school program. These individuals can be strong advocates for school library media programs. If these people can see that every effort is being made to deliver instruction of library media skills through an integrated program and that an effective job is being done in educating the young people of the community, a network for positive public relations is practically established.

When one thinks of library media services and the community, the first thing that comes to mind is the public library system. The public library is a source to be tapped by the school system. The library media supervisor can set the tone for the relationships between the public libraries and the schools. It is important for the library media supervisor and the director of public libraries in the district to confer on common problems and recommend solutions. These two individuals can best establish the kind of working relationship that should exist between the two institutions.

What kinds of schedules can be developed so that the local public librarian can know when the senior English class will be coming in to work on a research paper? How can the two institutions work together to plan for professional growth? What kinds of changes are occurring in the English (or social studies or science) curriculum that will impact on the public library? What networks are available through the public library that the school library media specialist should know about and be able to use? These are but a sampling of the issues that the two leaders should discuss in order to make the best possible use of the services that are available.

The library media supervisor needs to communicate with the central office administrative personnel—the superintendent's staff, the director of curriculum, the finance director, and anyone else in a decision-making position. Public relations skills are essential if the library media program is to get a liberal share of the budget and support from the key people in any school system. If the library media supervisor can effectively communicate that the library media program not only supports the entire curriculum in the district but also takes a primary role in teaching library media skills through an integrated curriculum process, then there is a firm base established for seeking support from the decision makers in the system. The central office professionals should be informed when the library media program in a school has been the key to improving scores on SAT tests. It should be informed when a student has done an outstanding piece of research in an English class by using the school library media center and the networking capabilities of the public library system. These key educational professionals should also be informed when things deteriorate because there has not been sufficient support.

It is usually the library media supervisor who makes the contact with individuals at the state department of education and then has the responsibility to communicate pertinent information to the specialist in the school. The personnel at the state level have the responsibility for establishing program guidelines, and they become liaisons with the local districts for implementation of those guidelines. The state library media supervisor can provide contact with other state supervisory personnel—the English supervisor, for example—and determine trends on a statewide basis. Through state offices, the local supervisor can make contact with other local supervisors and communicate needs, problems, and successful strategies. If professionals in leadership positions at the state level interpret and encourage library media skills in terms of integrated instruction, that influence will be felt in the local district. State library media services personnel seek input from the local supervisors, and often professional growth opportunities can be arranged through this vital source to further the professionalism of the school-based specialists. The district library media supervisor must make the other district personnel aware of the many services that can be offered through the state services: professional library services, networks for review and evaluation of materials, curriculum guides from a variety of districts across the country, and even nonprint sources that can be borrowed by the schools in the state. The implications for working with the state-based English personnel and library media personnel are monumental in terms of communication and cooperation.

In addition to state-based library media personnel, there are the various organizations that can provide material to help in the process of integrating skills. The nationally based American Library Association and the American Association of School Librarians produce quantities of valuable materials. There are smaller groups within these two affiliates that attack the questions of instruction in the library media centers across the nation. One such group is the Library Instruction Round Table, which addresses the instructional needs of librarians and library media specialists at all levels. The Association for Educational Communication and Technology is a vital national association for the library media specialist. In addition, there is the National Council of Teachers of English (NCTE), which is the organization for, by, and about English teachers. There are no rules that state that the library media supervisor cannot belong to the NCTE. It would be advantageous to belong to the appropriate organizations and benefit from the many newsletters, journals, conferences, and conventions that these organizations provide throughout the course of a year. The benefits would far outweigh the dollars spent for membership. Belonging to the organization of a fellow instructional leader lends validity to the role of the library media supervisor and sets an example to the school library that speaks to the interweaving of instructional roles.

There are usually local organizations to which the library media specialist should belong and be an active member that would include public library and school library media groups and English teachers' groups. One should investigate the possibilities for such organizations through the state department of education. Minimally, the library media supervisor should contact other instructional counterparts to be certain that the various publications from these organizations are shared. National concerns often are the same as local concerns, and one can take advantage of solutions to problems that may not have arrived at one's local district yet, or at the very least, take solace in the fact that other areas of the country are experiencing the same kinds of problems that are being experienced in the local district. These organizations exist for the benefit of their members, and there is a wealth of information to be gleaned from them. The knowledge that this information can be shared with others in the local district can often serve as a model to promote relationships and cooperation. Such organizations are extremely valuable resources for the library media supervisor (see Appendix 2).

THE SCHOOL LIBRARY MEDIA SPECIALIST
AND THE ENGLISH DEPARTMENT

The involvement of the English department chairperson is a vital factor in making the process of integrated skills work at the school level. It is important to win the confidence of this person and to let the person know the possibilities that exist for the English program in the library media center. Prior to any discussion with the English department chairperson, it is necessary for the library media specialist to have a good grasp of the various components of the English curriculum as it is taught in that particular school. One must keep in mind that when a curriculum is written at the district level, the schools within the district may not teach every course that is described in the district curriculum guide. The rationale for this is that offerings depend upon the school community, the specific school population, the strengths and limitations of the particular English department, and the number of students who indicate an interest in the course. It is imperative that the library media specialist be familiar with the school schedule and know exactly what English courses are being offered. Further, the specialist should know the course descriptions and the content of each course. The specialist also needs to know the personnel who are teaching the courses and what library media resources are available. In addition, a copy of the scope and sequence of library media skills should be available for the chairperson. With these things firmly in mind or in hand, the agenda for a meeting with the English department chairperson should include:

1. Schedule:

    - Who in the English department is teaching what courses and when?

    - Where can the library media specialist most logically plug into that schedule for orientation with the incoming freshman class?

    - Which courses will require research projects and when?

    - What kinds of resources will be needed?

    - What kinds of instruction from library media services will be needed?

    - How can this instruction fit into the scope and sequence of library media skills?

    - What classes will be required to do supplemental reading and what kinds of reserve collections or bibliographic assistance will be needed to facilitate that reading?

    - What classes would logically need to schedule television facilities or other kinds of production facilities within the school building and under the jurisdiction of the library media center?

2. Goals and Objectives:

- What is the English department chairperson's interpretation of the objectives of the English program in this school, based on state guidelines and district goals?

- How can the goals and objectives for the library media program mesh with these interpretations?

- How can the two departments work together to implement those goals?

- What kinds of activities were completed successfully in the past by the two departments? Unsuccessfully?

- What can be done by the library media specialist to improve services to assist in meeting those objectives?

3. Resources:

- What resources are available in print and nonprint materials in the school library media center to assist in the overall teaching of the English department?

- What resources need to be reserved through district services, for example, a film or videocassette library? Can a schedule be established in advance to assure that the teachers will get what they need when they can make the most effective use of the material?

- What resources will need to be obtained from the community? Public library? What outside production services are available?

- Is it possible to send a schedule regarding research projects to the public library to help the library prepare for the onslaught of students who have a project due tomorrow or next week?

- Are there courses that could take advantage of a file of speakers from the community, and can these individuals be scheduled in advance?

- How can microcomputers housed in the library media center best be used by English classes?

4. Activities:

- What activities are planned to utilize the facilities of the school library media center's production facilities or limited kinds of equipment?

- What activities are planned that will use the space in the library media center, and how can those activities best be scheduled?

- Are there activities planned that will require the use of stations, and what assistance from the library media program can be given in creation of those stations?

- Are there group activities that will need to be scheduled at the same time as other groups, and what provisions can be made to avoid undue confusion?

This list is by no means exhaustive, but it is a starting point for dialogue between the library media specialist and the English department chairperson. The questions themselves let the chairperson know that the library media center is a force to be reckoned with—and not missed!

The purpose of any discussion with the department chairperson is to create a relationship that will foster the use of the library media center by the members of the English teaching staff. The chairperson becomes the catalyst through whom the library media specialist can work to reach the other teachers in the department. The library media specialist may wish to speak with the entire English department at once in order to suggest the kinds of things that can be done together, but it is essential that each teacher be met with on an individual basis in order to work through a skills integration package. To be realistic, it may be possible to reach only one or two teachers in a single department in a year, but the word will spread with each successful experience and relationships will become established. In order to accomplish these successful experiences, another component of good public relations comes into play—careful planning.

In his book, *Managing the Building-Level School Library Media Program*, Warren B. Hicks lists seven steps to be used for any planning process.

1. Identify the problems and recognize opportunities.

2. Set initial objectives.

3. Determine the planning premises—frame the appropriate courses of action, examine data, examine objectives and their alternatives, select the best alternatives for implementation, and decide on courses of action to meet these objectives.

4. Review the alternative courses of action—all courses of action should be investigated.

5. Evaluate each course of action in terms of problems to be solved and the objective to be achieved.

6. Select a plan of action to be implemented.

7. Implement the plan.

In reference to the final step in the planning process, Hicks writes: "The total management process comes into play at this step and the media manager uses all of the functions, tools and techniques available to construct the support and implementation systems to carry out the plan." He also stresses the importance of evaluating the plan after it is implemented and revising as necessary.[1]

The importance of good planning cannot be overstated. Obviously, there are times when creative things occur spontaneously, but given the load carried by the library media specialist and the English teacher, the chances for such occurrences are rare because they simply will not fit into a crowded schedule.

It is essential that the library media specialist plan with the new English teacher in the department. Time should be made for an orientation session with all new staff members to the library media center. The new English teacher needs to know the kinds of services that are readily obtainable from the school library media center and from district services. The new member of the staff can often provide the golden opportunity for demonstrating ways in which programs can be integrated; the new person is most likely to appreciate any help that is offered. It is equally important to plan carefully with the English teachers who will be teaching students new to the school. An orientation schedule must be established that will allow time for assessing every student's entry level in library media skills. Even if a school system is fortunate enough to have a well-established scope and sequence of library media skills, it is important to know exactly what needs to be reviewed, retaught, and introduced. Students become quickly bored and teachers become impatient when classes are taught things they already know. On the other hand, nothing can be more deadly than working with a class when the library media specialist has erroneously assumed that the students have the necessary prerequisite information. The instructor may as well be speaking to the students in an unknown tongue. Plan, then, with the English teacher to pretest all incoming students in the area of library media skills.

In addition to discussing the library media program with the English department chairperson, the library media specialist should discuss schedules, goals and objectives, resources, and activities with each teacher in the English department. It should be encouraging to note that once this has taken place, ongoing relationships do not need to take enormous amounts of time. Brief communications are usually adequate. The English teacher needs to have realistic expectations of the library media program, and it is easier if those expectations can be established before the fact. For example, the English department should know that it cannot assign the same title to every student in a class and expect them all to have access to that title from the library media collection. As a rule, the library media collection will carry multiple copies of popular books that may be assigned—perhaps five copies would be the limit. The English teacher needs to know that the collection does not hold thirty-five copies of *A Separate Peace* or any other book used as a text. The English teacher also needs to know that the specialist can provide many other titles on the subject of adolescence and youth.

If the library media center has bought into one of the online reference systems for the microcomputer, the English teacher needs to know exactly what the constraints are with regard to the search process. Time must be allotted for the student to learn to do a search and investigate ways in which to access the materials that are indicated. More and more library media centers are purchasing data banks of information in the format of microcomputer software in lieu of print copies. Scores of management tools make demands on every available microprocessor. The microcomputer housed in the library media center could also be used as a word processing unit for the English department. If the library media specialist is having a bibliography updated on the microcomputer when an English student comes in to use it, there will be a conflict and a sense that the library media specialist just talks a good line. Communication and planning are important considerations when someone needs to use specialized equipment, particularly equipment with the versatility of the microcomputer.

THE LIBRARY MEDIA SPECIALIST
AND SCHOOL ADMINISTRATORS

In order for any school library media program to be a successful one, the library media specialist must build relationships with the school administration. The principal of the high school should be informed if the library media program is going to begin to implement an integrated skills program with the English department. One thing that this writer has discovered through many years of classroom and library media center experience is that principals do not like surprises. The administrator deserves to be kept informed about what is happening in the school. The specialist needs the principal's support for any new venture and needs to supply him or her with the necessary information to provide that support. The specialist and the principal need to discuss such questions as: What time elements must be built into a schedule if the library media specialist is going to work on integrating skills with the English department in the school or at the district level? How can planning time be arranged to suit both the library media specialist and the members of the English department if skills must be matched at the school level? What help can be provided to the English department and the library media center if a quantity of typing and duplicating is necessary? In summary, the specialist and the principal must work together. The library media specialist can hardly insist that preplanning and scheduling of the center's space be done ahead of time if there is no support from the instructional leader in the school.

THE LIBRARY MEDIA SPECIALIST
AND THE PUBLIC LIBRARY

Taking the lead from the library media supervisor in the district, the school library media specialist must reach out to the nearest public library staff. On a personal basis, the needs of the English department can be effectively communicated. The specialist should invite the public librarian into the school for an orientation to the school's library media center. The two should discuss common problems and goals and discover ways in which the two services can best accommodate the school population. The school library media specialist should be well acquainted with the resources, the rules and regulations, and the personnel of the local branch of the public library. That information can in turn be communicated to the staff and students in the school and make their contacts with the public librarians worthwhile. The specialist can use the steps suggested in Hicks's planning model to provide a duality of service for the school population.

All of the groups mentioned under the heading The School Library Media Supervisor should become a part of the relationships formed by the school-based library personnel: the community, the state department of education, and various central office personnel as appropriate. The important thing is for the specialist to stress the positive image of library media services within the school, particularly as the specialist proceeds with the integration of library media skills into a particular facet of the curriculum.

It is not the intent of this book to illustrate all the ways in which the student should be reached by the library media specialist. But it should be noted that the student is considered in everything the specialist does. After all, the purpose for schools is to provide learning opportunities for students, and students and learning are why library media specialists, teachers, principals, and supervisors have jobs. Every relationship created by the library media specialist should be for the benefit of the students. The specialist should never be so busy with the tactics of the job as to forget the reason for being there in the first place.

As the library media supervisors or specialists work at building relationships through communication, planning, and other components of a public relations program, they clear the way for delivering an integrated program of library media skills and English curriculum skills.

NOTES

[1] Warren Hicks, *Managing the Building-Level School Library Media Program.* (Chicago: American Library Association, 1981), 17.

BIBLIOGRAPHY ON LIBRARY MEDIA SPECIALISTS AND PUBLIC RELATIONS ACTIVITIES

Angoff, Allan, ed. *Public Relations for Libraries: Essays in Communications Techniques.* Westport, Conn.: Greenwood Press, 1973.

Baeckler, Virginia. *Sparkle: PR for Library Staff.* Hopewell, N.J.: Sources, 1980.

Baeckler, Virginia, and Linda Larson. *Go, Pep and Pop: Two Hundred Fifty Tested Ideas for Lively Libraries.* New York: UNABASHED Librarian, 1976.

Coursen, David. "Communicating." In *School Leadership: Handbook for Survival,* edited by Stuart C. Smith, JoAnn Mazzarella, and Philip K. Piele, 194-214. Eugene, Oreg.: University of Oregon, 1981.

Davies, Ruth. *The School Library Media Program: Instructional Force for Excellence,* 359-78. New York: R. R. Bowker Company, 1979.

Garvey, Mona. *Library Public Relations.* New York: H. W. Wilson, 1980.

Kohn, Rita, and Krysta Tepper. *You Can Do It: A PR Skills Manual for Librarians.* Metuchen, N.J.: Scarecrow Press, Inc., 1981.

Kohn, Rita, and Krysta Tepper. *Have You Got What They Want? Public Relation Strategies for the School Library Media Specialist.* Metuchen, N.J.: Scarecrow Press, Inc., 1982.

Taggart, Dorothy T. *Management and Administration of the School Library Media Program,* 11-23. Hamden, Conn.: Shoe String Press, Inc., 1980.

5

Scope and Sequence
of Skills

One of the most important tools used by the library media specialist in the school is the scope and sequence of skills for library media studies. The development of such a tool relies heavily upon what occurs in other areas of the curriculum; the library media program needs to be synchronized with what is required in English skills, social studies skills, or science skills. If curriculum is written at the district level, the scope and sequence of library media skills should be developed at the district level. Doing so permits communication with key people in other subject areas and creates an easier flow for plugging in the proper skill at the proper level. If a scope and sequence of skills is developed at the school level, it is equally important that people from each department be contacted to assure that library media instruction is built into subject area schedules, especially if research or production facilities will be required at a specific time. At the elementary level, the library media specialist would teach the rudiments of the card catalog after alphabetizing skills have been taught. At the secondary level, the specialist would introduce the variety of reference sources available in the school library media center before students are required to write research papers.

Because a scope and sequence of skills exists, it does not mean that every student absorbs all of the necessary skills in each particular grade level. It is common practice for the classroom teacher to give diagnostic tests at the beginning of the school year to establish exactly what the students know. From such a test, the teacher can then determine what needs to be reviewed and what needs to be retaught. The practice of administering a diagnostic test to incoming students should be part of the routine of the library media specialist. There are commercial tests available, but the library media specialist can create a very simple test to address those things that have been problem areas in the past. Administering such a test should be a brief part of the orientation program. The scope and sequence document serves as the teaching guide for orderly, logical learning on the part of the student.

A scope and sequence of library media skills gives validity to the teaching aspect of the library media specialist. The specialist can say to a teacher, "According to your schedule you will be teaching a unit on biography in February. Our library media skills scope and sequence indicates that we are responsible for the instruction on how to locate biographies. Suppose we schedule your class for the library media center for that purpose." If the specialist can present such a plan to the teacher, then the teacher will more readily accept the role of the library media specialist as fellow teacher. The library media specialist is saying to the teacher, "You have to do this with your class; this is part of what I can do to help you accomplish your task, and a scope and sequence says I am supposed to do it."

The development of a scope and sequence of skills in any discipline is a complicated and time-consuming task. Since library media skills must take into account the skills sequence in every other subject area, it becomes even more arduous. In chapter 3, there is a brief discussion on the process of developing curriculum using the committee method. Using a committee of library media personnel and knowledgeable individuals from other curriculum areas is probably the most efficient way to develop a library media skills scope and sequence. Fortunately, there are many excellent, tested documents in place in school library media centers that may aid the developers of a scope and sequence. State departments of education frequently have copies of a variety of curriculum documents that may be borrowed to use as guides for the work of a particular district or school. Conferences and literature from the organizations mentioned in chapter 4 can be excellent sources for obtaining information from other districts and schools.

WISCONSIN LIBRARY MEDIA SKILLS GUIDE

One state that has a library media skills guide in place is the state of Wisconsin. The Wisconsin School Library Media Association developed the *Wisconsin Library Media Skills Guide* as "a starting point from which a program can be adapted to fit a local situation."[1] The thrust of the Wisconsin guide is the integration of library media skills into the instructional program. In the introduction to this document, it states: "It should be stressed that the development of a school's program and the responsibility for instruction must be shared by teachers and media specialists. Students must see a need for mastering and using media skills as part of their classroom instruction."[2] The library media skills are divided into five major categories:

- Orientation

- Organization and Utilization of Resources

- Selection of Resources

- Research and Study Skills

- Production and Utilization of Materials

These skills are broken down by grade level, and procedures, including objectives, activities, resources, evaluation, and curricular applications are carefully developed. This document, which was developed by a committee consisting of personnel from the University of Wisconsin at La Crosse and Whitewater and from school and district level library media services, is available from the Wisconsin Library Association, 1922 University Avenue, Madison, Wisconsin 53705. Anyone wishing to receive the document, which covers a scope and sequence of library skills for kindergarten through grade twelve, should write to the Wisconsin Library

Association (under whose auspices the School Library Media Association functions) for the cost of the skills guide. It should be noted that other states have developed similar tools; Pennsylvania, Alaska, and Hawaii are but a few examples.

ANNE ARUNDEL COUNTY, MARYLAND
SCOPE AND SEQUENCE OF LIBRARY MEDIA SKILLS

Library Media Skills—Scope and Sequence is a document developed at the district level through the auspices of Library Media Services for the Anne Arundel County Public Schools. Anne Arundel County is a local school district in the state of Maryland. This guide is printed for the school system in booklet form and in chart form. The latter enables the user to see the broad scope of skills at a glance and facilitates integrating skills into the curriculum. Again, library media skills are divided into five major categories:

- Orientation

- Location and Selection

- Utilization and Comprehension

- Knowledge of and Appreciation for Literature and Reading

- Production

Skills to be taught are listed in terms of student objectives under specific grade levels—kindergarten through grade twelve. Each skill is repeated under each level, in the belief that reinforcement and practice are necessary if the student is to become an independent user of library media services. The skills to be introduced at a particular level are underlined. Careful consideration was given to other curriculum documents during the development of this tool. This consideration makes it easier for the school-based library media specialist to integrate skills into the instructional program. A reprint of the Anne Arundel County scope and sequence of library media skills for grades nine through twelve follows.

=·=·=·=·=·=·=

INSTRUCTIONAL OBJECTIVES FOR LIBRARY MEDIA SKILLS, GRADES NINE THROUGH TWELVE

Grade Nine

ORIENTATION

The student will:

Demonstrate a knowledge of procedures.

Identify personnel and library media center hours.

Check-out and return of materials.

Care of books.

Care of nonbook materials.

Observe appropriate conduct.

Demonstrate knowledge of emergency evacuation procedures.

Demonstrate consideration for others.

Return library media center materials, equipment, and furniture before leaving center.

LOCATION AND SELECTION

The student will:

Locate important features of the library media center.

Check-out desk/book return.

Card catalog.

Reference section.

Microform reader/printer and microform collection (if available).

Career Center (if available).

TV studio (if available).

Dark room and Media Production room (if available).

Other.

Locate books and nonbook materials by the Dewey Decimal System.

Book and nonbook catalog cards.

The subject, title, and author cards in the card catalog.

Fiction and nonfiction materials by call number.

Magazines and newspapers.

Vertical file materials.

Career materials.

Reprinted, by permission, from Library Media Services, Anne Arundel County Public Schools, *Library Media Skills—Scope and Sequence* (Annapolis, Md.: Anne Arundel County Public Schools, 1978).

LOCATION AND SELECTION (cont'd)

Locate the nearest public library.

Select books and nonbook materials for personal enjoyment and/or specific purposes.

UTILIZATION AND COMPREHENSION

The student will:

Use the card catalog as an index to the library media center collection.

Guide letters on the front of drawers.

Alphabetical filing system.

Contents of the subject card, title card, and author card to find the call number and bibliographic information.

Cross reference cards.

Alphabetical and/or chronological arrangement of subject cards.

Identify in books:

Author	Title page and verso
Title	Publisher
Call number	Copyright date
Table of contents	Appendix
Index	Foreword/preface
Glossary	Bibliography

Identify in nonbook materials:

Title

Call number

Types

Record	Chart
Tape	Filmloop
Slide	Film
Kit	Transparency
Filmstrip	

Others as available (video tape, computer software, microform, etc.)

Demonstrate ability to use:

Record player

Listening station

Filmstrip viewer/projector

Filmloop projector

Cassette tape player/recorder

Overhead projector

Slide previewer/projector

16mm projector

Sound filmstrip viewer/projector

Opaque projector

Reel-to-reel tape recorder
Other equipment as available (card reader, still camera, super 8mm camera/projector, Visual Maker, Thermofax transparency maker, video camera/recorder/monitor/receiver, microcomputer, microform reader, etc.

Extend skills in using general reference materials:
Almanacs
Dictionaries (inc. *Thesaurus*)
Indexes (inc. *Readers' Guide*)
Atlases
Public library catalogs
Other special reference books as needed

Use newspapers, magazines, and vertical file material as a source of information, using the format and arrangement as a guide to contents.

Use a bibliography to identify further information on a specific topic.

Demonstrate knowledge of the parts of a book used in locating information.

Use audiovisual materials as a source of information.

Consider criteria for judging materials in terms of usefulness.

KNOWLEDGE OF AND APPRECIATION FOR LITERATURE AND READING

The student will:
Recognize a variety of book types:
Fiction
Short stories
Science fiction
Nonfiction, as appropriate.

Participate in book talk activities.

Choose reading as a leisure time activity.

Satisfy individual interests by selecting reading material relevant to interests, purposes, and/or abilities.

Choose fiction materials relating to curriculum units.

PRODUCTION

The student will:
Produce audiovisual materials, such as:
Tape recordings
Visuals using the opaque/overhead projectors
Handmade and/or thermal transparencies
Presentations with pictures using slides or photographs

PRODUCTION (cont'd)

Produce audiovisual materials, such as: (cont'd)

Slide/tape presentations
Sound filmstrip presentations
Super 8 mm film and/or video tapes

Become aware of the suitability of particular media forms for specific purposes, and select the most appropriate to communicate content or creative ideas.

Grades Ten through Twelve

ORIENTATION

The student will:

Demonstrate a knowledge of procedures.
Identify personnel and library media center hours.
Check-out and return of materials.
Care of books.
Care of nonbook materials.

Observe appropriate conduct.
Demonstrate knowledge of emergency evacuation procedures.
Demonstrate consideration of others.
Return library media center materials, equipment, and furniture before leaving center.

LOCATION AND SELECTION

The student will:

Locate important features of the library media center.
Check-out desk/book return.
Card catalog.
Reference section.
Microform reader/printer and microform collection.
Microcomputer and software collection.
TV Studio (if available).
Dark room and Media Production room (if available).
Other.

Locate books and nonbook materials by the Dewey Decimal System.
Book and nonbook catalog cards.
The subject, title, and author cards in the card catalog.
Fiction and nonfiction materials by call number.
Magazines and newspapers.
Vertical file materials.
Career materials.

Locate the nearest public library.

Select books and nonbook materials for personal enjoyment and/ or specific purposes.

UTILIZATION AND COMPREHENSION

The student will:

Use the card catalog as an index to the library media center collection.

Contents of the subject card, title card, and author card to find the call number and bibliographic information.

Cross reference cards.

Alphabetical and/or chronological arrangement of subject cards.

Identify in books:

Author	Title page and verso
Title	Publisher
Call number	Copyright date
Table of contents	Appendix
Index	Foreword/preface
Glossary	Bibliography

Identify in nonbook materials:

Title

Call number

Types

Record	Chart
Tape	Filmloop
Slide	Film
Kit	Transparency
Filmstrip	

Others as available (video tape, computer software, microform, etc.)

Demonstrate ability to use:

Record player

Listening station

Filmstrip viewer/projector

Filmloop projector

Cassette tape player/recorder

Overhead projector

Slide previewer/projector

16mm projector

Sound filmstrip viewer/projector

Opaque projector

Reel-to-reel tape recorder

Other equipment as available (card reader, still camera, super 8 mm camera/projector, Visual Maker, Thermofax transparency maker, video camera/recorder/monitor/ receiver, microcomputer, microform reader, etc.)

UTILIZATION AND COMPREHENSION (cont'd)

Extend skills in utilizing <u>all available</u> reference materials, as appropriate:

Encyclopedias (identifying purpose, scope, and limitations)
Almanacs
Dictionaries (inc. *Thesaurus*)
Indexes (inc. *Readers' Guide*)
Atlases <u>and gazetteers</u>
Public library catalogs
Other special reference books as needed.

Use newspapers, magazines, and vertical file material as a source of information, using the format and arrangement as a guide to contents.

Use a bibliography to identify further information on a specific topic.

Use audiovisual materials as a source of information.

Evaluate materials in terms of usefulness.

KNOWLEDGE OF AND APPRECIATION FOR LITERATURE AND READING

The student will:

Recognize a variety of book types.
Fiction and nonfiction, as appropriate.

Participate in book talk activities.

Choose reading as a leisure time activity.

Satisfy individual interests by selecting reading material relevant to interests, purposes, and/or abilities.

PRODUCTION

The student will:

Produce audiovisual materials <u>as appropriate, using full resources of the library media center.</u>

Become aware of the suitability of particular media forms for specific purposes and select the <u>most appropriate</u> to communicate content or creative ideas.

≡·≡·≡·≡·≡·≡·≡

BALTIMORE COUNTY, MARYLAND
SCOPE AND SEQUENCE OF ENGLISH SKILLS

In chapter 3, reference was made to the use of scope and sequence for developing curriculum and for its importance in terms of "horizontal articulation." Thus, it would seem appropriate to include a scope and sequence for English skills. The scope and sequence that follows is an overview of the entire English curriculum, grades nine through twelve, developed by the Baltimore Public Schools, a local school system in Maryland. In this document, the dash used before each objective represents the words *the student will be able.*

≡·≡·≡·≡·≡·≡

AN OVERVIEW OF INSTRUCTIONAL OBJECTIVES IN COMPOSING, INTERPRETING, AND LANGUAGE, GRADES NINE THROUGH TWELVE

Composing Exposition

GRADE NINE

—To present an oral or written report which classifies information gathered from some type of research.

—To write a short essay analyzing the particular quality of similar television programs.

GRADE TEN

—To show the relationship between one element of a fictional dramatic narrative and the work as a whole in an oral or written analysis arranged either inductively or deductively.

—To organize and assemble information in a written report intended for a specific audience.

—To analyze the possible organizational patterns that a response to an "essay question" might take, and to select one pattern to develop in response to the question.

Reprinted, by permission, from the English Office, Division of Instruction, Baltimore County Public Schools, *An Overview of Instructional Objectives in Composing, Interpreting, and Language, Grades 7-12* (Towson, Md.: Baltimore County Public Schools, 1975).

GRADE ELEVEN

—To compare and contrast, in writing, orally, or in a mixed verbal-nonverbal form, the views of two actual persons or characters from American literature who represent opposing or different values in American life, past and/or present.

—To select a problem in contemporary American life that has been a problem in the past, and to trace the changes in attitudes and solutions to the problem from some time in the past up to the present, as the problem is reflected in American literature.

GRADE TWELVE

—To present the results of independent inquiry in a written, oral, or mixed media (verbal and nonverbal) report.

—To write an extended definition of an abstract term related to the study of a universal theme in literature, an archetypal character, or an ethnic or cultural prototype.

Interpreting Exposition

GRADE NINE

—To determine ways in which a generalization can be supported with concrete narrative illustrations.

—To identify the details and means of presentation by which an "image" of a public celebrity is projected by the mass media.

GRADE TEN

—To gather information for a report through one or more types of investigation based on first-hand observation, a variety of library resources, and/or interviews.

—To relate the way a topic is treated (selection, organization, and development) to the limitations and possibilities of a particular medium used to convey information.

GRADE ELEVEN

—To infer from an analysis of television programming the values appealed to by products and/or advertisers.

—To locate, take notes on, and organize information needed by you or a group of students in class as background to the study of American life and literature.

GRADE TWELVE

—To locate and outline examples of several types of paragraph or chapter organizations used in printed material of a basically expository nature; and to cite ways that transitional devices, initial sentences of paragraphs or sentences, types of supporting material, and arrangement of detail typify a specific type of organizational pattern.

—To locate factual information on a particular topic by identifying and using sources appropriate to the topic and by developing methods of investigation suitable for the topic.

—To identify and give examples of underlying expository patterns of materials presented in mixed verbal-nonverbal or entirely non-verbal media; and relate these patterns to those commonly used in expository writing.

—To explain the way in which the use of a particular medium for an expository "message" causes adjustment in the types of transitions, beginnings, and developmental details because of the nature of the medium (code) itself.

Composing Expressions of Opinion

GRADE NINE

—To express a positive or negative reaction to the portrayal of two characters who appear in different works.

—To agree or disagree, orally or in writing, with a given assertion or with a statement formulated by the class, the teacher, or by a writer expressing an opinion through television or news media.

—To express a personal preference for one person, object, or form of entertainment over another and to support this preference with explanatory detail.

GRADE TEN

—To defend a personal conviction about the author's or producer's treatment of a theme in a literary work or film.

—To develop a position on a controversial issue and support it through research.

GRADE ELEVEN

—To express an opinion about a particular work by an American writer or producer.

GRADE ELEVEN (cont'd)

—To write a critical review in the form of a short personal essay or a "professional" type review, of one or more works by an American writer, artist, or song writer.

GRADE TWELVE

—To take a position in regard to a serious personal decision as to its ethical or cultural "rightness" or "wrongness."

Interpreting Expressions of Opinion

GRADE NINE

—To analyze the structure and purpose of a critical review, an essay, or a continuing newspaper or television commentary.

—To identify the bias of an article and to explain the methods and purposes of "slanting" that are used.

GRADE TEN

—To recognize persuasive devices and techniques in advertisements.

—To analyze the validity of written arguments presented in a variety of forms and media.

GRADE ELEVEN

—To analyze rhetorical devices in famous American speeches.

—To analyze the use of rhetorical devices in works by American writers.

—To examine the various types of critical comment to induce the types of support and rhetorical devices most effective for persuasion and argument.

GRADE TWELVE

—To examine in communication persuasive discourse of various types.

—To use reviews written by professional critics, reviewers, or feature columnists as a guide to the selection of films, television programs, recordings, art exhibits, concerts, or reading material in which you would be interested.

Composing Prose and Dramatic Narratives

GRADE NINE

—To clarify the meaning of a particular personal experience with a similar experience of another person.

—To create an original situation and dialogue consistent with an established characterization in a story, novel, or biography.

—To write a description of a natural scene or an indoor setting, adopting the point of view of an observer who is moving past or through the place he describes.

GRADE TEN

—To convert point of view from first person to third person.

—To develop a conflict in dialogue that leads to a climax.

—To compose a monologue from a character's point of view.

GRADE ELEVEN

—To narrate a series of events involving you and another person that make that person memorable in your life.

—To invent and develop a situation for a character from American fiction or drama.

—To convert a portion of a narrative into a news story or to convert a news story into a portion of a narrative after comparing the treatment of narrative elements in expository narratives and in literary narratives, both fictional and nonfictional.

GRADE TWELVE

—To develop an incident from personal experience into a short-short story or personal essay which evokes either a comic or sympathetic reader-reaction.

—To develop a narrative based on an imaginary character in a specified "non-American" cultural setting.

Interpreting Prose and Dramatic Narratives

GRADE NINE

—To understand that in both fiction and nonfiction, authors carefully select details to create the desired image of a character.

—To observe ways in which universal or recurrent themes are treated in various genres.

GRADE NINE (cont'd)

—To observe ways by which narrative material is adapted from one medium to another.

GRADE TEN

—To differentiate between general themes and specific aspects of general themes in literature and to understand that a work often treats more than one general theme.

—To recognize the result of a choice of a certain point of view on the reader's perception of a series of narrative events.

—To recognize the relationship between the narrative elements and production elements of a play.

GRADE ELEVEN

—To compare treatment of similar general themes within narratives of one historical period or two different periods.

—To recognize individual marks of an American writer's style.

—To understand the deviations from the conventions of "realistic" drama of some American playwrights.

GRADE TWELVE

—To demonstrate an understanding of the narrative elements in drama by choosing production elements which are consistent with the playwright's treatment of the narrative elements.

—To interpret the basic types of conflict characteristic in long or short fiction and to demonstrate how the plot is a series of events related to the resolution of a particular conflict.

—To read and interpret in terms of plot, character, setting, or any other element of fiction, a short story which is unfamiliar.

Composing Poetry

GRADE NINE

—To convert sensory impressions first into a descriptive paragraph and then into a short poem.

—To create sensory images through a nonprint presentation to accompany an oral reading of a poem.

GRADE TEN

—To compose a poem which develops a particular meaning, feeling, or "theme."

—To express in poetic form a new view of a familiar object.

GRADE ELEVEN

—To write in verse form an extended definition of a universal feeling or abstract idea using a series of concrete images or a "catalog" of objects, events, impressions to develop the definition.

—To compose a poem in a contemporary/experimental form of your own choice that uses as subject matter a reaction to some contemporary American goal or value.

GRADE TWELVE

—To write a poem in a deliberately chosen form where the impetus for topic, mood, or idea arises from any of the Grade 12 units.

Interpreting Poetry

GRADE NINE

—To determine how the poet elicits sensory responses through the use of imagery and other devices.

—To discover the function of connotation in transmitting the "meanings" or feelings of a poem.

GRADE TEN

—To identify the points of view in narrative and dramatic poetry and state the advantages or possible reasons for selection of the chosen point of view.

—To interpret poems with several layers or "levels" of meaning (literal, philosophical, sociological, psychological).

GRADE ELEVEN

—To determine how the form and content of poetry reflect American cultural attitudes.

—To become familiar with the characteristics of a particular American poet.

GRADE TWELVE

—To interpret a fairly simple poem, unfamiliar to you, on a literal level; and to describe any other aspects of meaning that may arise from tone, theme, imagery, diction, or rhythmic patterns.

The Nature of Language

GRADE NINE

—To recognize the various types of figurative language in discourse and explain the use of figurative language in relating an experience or idea more vividly.

—To understand that all figurative language is based on comparisons of essentially dissimilar items.

GRADE TEN

—To understand that meaning is frequently communicated nonverbally, either exclusively or in combination with language, and that both forms of a communication share language principles.

GRADE ELEVEN

—To identify difficulties in comprehension of certain American writers and to attempt to relate these to differences between the writer's and reader's use of language.

GRADE TWELVE

—To recognize and cite examples of influences most responsible for the growth and development of the English language.

—To use the dictionary as a source of information about changes in the English language.

≡·≡·≡·≡·≡·≡·≡

The library media specialist in the senior high school who takes a close look at the overview of the English program on the foregoing pages will readily see places where the library media program could play an important role. When the specialist begins to match those elements of the English program with the elements found in the library media skills scope and sequence, then the process of integrating curriculum is set in motion. Two matched elements might be written as one and implemented as one objective with two parts, with the library media specialist taking one part and the English teacher taking the other. For example, in grade ten, one English objective is *to gather information for a report through one or more types of investigation based on first-hand observation, a variety of library resources, and/or interviews.* In grades ten through twelve, in a library media skills scope and sequence, one objective is *the student will extend skills in utilization and comprehension of all available reference materials.* The combined objective could read: *The student will gather information for a report through one or more types of investigation based on first-hand observation, interviews, and/or a variety of library resources after appropriate instruction/review of available library media resources has been conducted through the library media specialist.* This last objective covers both programs and assures that the library media specialist will have input for the benefit of the students in reaching the particular objective. Some examples of how this has worked in actual practice will be given in following chapters.

NOTES

[1] Wisconsin School Library Media Association, *Wisconsin Library Media Skills Guide* (Madison, Wis.: Wisconsin Library Association, 1979).

[2] Ibid.

6

District Level Integration of Skills

In chapter 3, there is a discussion of the process involved in writing curriculum and the ways in which the library media specialist can have input and develop the format for skills integration. Since all curricula are not rewritten every year, this opportunity is one that must be seized when and if the actual writing occurs. Many school systems or individual schools have courses of study in place. For the purpose of this book, and specifically this chapter, the writer will approach curriculum that is in place and written at the district level. There is no reason why the same ideas could not be applied to school level courses of study.

SKILLS INTEGRATION PROCESS FOR AN EXISTING CURRICULUM

Given a particular course of study in English and the scope and sequence of library media skills, it is possible to develop a match of skills and allocate certain aspects of the existing course of study in English to the library media program. If an English objective states that the student will write a report on the quality of current films using three magazine articles, it is obvious that library media services come into the picture. Certain questions need to be answered. Do the students need a review on how to use *The Readers' Guide to Periodical Literature*? How much time needs to be scheduled in the library media center for research? Do the students understand the process for getting periodicals and the circulation restrictions? A committee should be formed consisting of library media specialists, English teachers, and appropriate supervisory staff to develop such a match of skills. A complete scope and sequence can then be published and used by all of the high schools in the system. While this is an after-the-fact approach, it does the job, and practicality wins the day.

One school system that integrated instruction in library media skills and the English program is Prince George's County Public Schools.

SKILLS INTEGRATION PROCESS
IN PRINCE GEORGE'S COUNTY, MARYLAND

The budgetary cutbacks that most school systems have suffered are probably exemplified by the situation that exists in Prince George's County, Maryland. Prince George's County is a large school system whose borders include large portions of a metropolitan area and some rural areas, and it is adjacent to a wealthy county. Since 1980, Prince George's County has had to close sixty-eight schools. Concurrent with school closings has been the dilemma of reduction in force (RIF), a situation that has mightily affected the school library media program. In the late seventies, this county's library media program was considered exemplary and its staff enviable. It was a model for many in the state of Maryland and elsewhere. With the RIF's and severe budget problems affecting this local school system, there was a terrible impact on the morale of the library media staff. The library media leadership in Prince George's County, coordinated by the supervisor, refused to provide fewer library media services to the schools. Instead, they consolidated central office services and, among other things, developed a document called *Integrating the Library Skills Program into the Language Arts Curriculum, 7-12.*

In its introduction, this document states:

> The purpose of this document is to demonstrate the integration of a variety of library media center skills and resources into the language arts curriculum. The fusion of these two curricular areas benefits the teachers and students by enhancing classroom instruction and providing a greater selection of educational materials. For optimum success, the essential element is cooperative planning between the library media specialist and the language arts teacher. Suggested guidelines are included to facilitate this joint effort.
>
> For each grade level 7-12, two units were selected from the language arts curriculum guides. Each unit includes a list of suggested activities which provides opportunities for career exploration, media production and research. Two detailed lesson plans for each unit demonstrate how library media skills can be incorporated into a language arts lesson. These activities may be adapted to various ability levels and other grade levels. Specific resources mentioned may not be available in all library media centers; however, substitutions or adaptations may be easily made.*

---

*Reprinted by permission of Dr. Edward Barth, Supervisor, Office of Library and Media Services, Palmer Park Service Center. From Prince George's County Public Schools, *Integrating the Library Skills Program into the Language Arts Curriculum, 7-12.* (Landover, Md.: Prince George's County Public Schools, 1983).

The committee that worked on the skills integration process for this document included library media staff members, English staff members, and the reading supervisor, as well as a team of middle school professionals. Emphasis was placed on the fact that for optimum success, cooperative planning is essential between the library media specialist and the language arts teacher in the specific school. This guide was developed for district-wide use; it demonstrates what can be done in the skills integration area, and it indicates that other subject areas can be integrated following its recommendations and examples. The process used by the professional personnel in Prince George's County demonstrates how two subject areas can be integrated after curriculum is already in place. The following material is reprinted from the guide. First is the set of guidelines for the consultation between the language arts teacher and library media specialist. Second is the list of components of a daily lesson. Third is a plan for an integrated objective for nonfiction at the ninth grade level. Fourth is a plan for an integrated objective for history of language at the twelfth grade level.

≡·≡·≡·≡·≡·≡·≡

GUIDELINES FOR LANGUAGE ARTS TEACHER/ LIBRARY MEDIA SPECIALIST CONSULTATION

1. A convenient time for both professionals to meet should be arranged. (Meeting times do not have to be long!)

2. Language arts teacher or library media specialist describes topic idea being considered (include time frame, level, and number of students.)

3. Both teachers brainstorm ideas for student activities.

4. The initial activity strateg/ is decided. The activity may be classroom or media center oriented.

5. At the end of the first meeting, a time for follow-up is scheduled.

Reprinted by permission of Dr. Edward Barth, Supervisor, Office of Library and Media Services, Palmer Park Service Center. From Prince George's County Public Schools, *Integrating the Library Skills Program into the Language Arts Curriculum, 7-12*. (Landover, Md.: Prince George's County Public Schools, 1983).

6. Library media specialist meets with the language arts teacher (or sends note) at the pre-arranged follow-up time, detailing the results of his/her search (include availability of resources in the library media center and the community, special collections, or other materials gathered, etc.)

7. The language arts teacher and the library media specialist refine the activity, set targets, and divide responsibilities (who does what, who teaches what skill, location of teaching, grouping of students, etc.)

8. Library media specialist and the language arts teacher may schedule appropriate time(s) in the library media center and note in plan books when (if) the library media specialist should come to the classroom.

9. The language arts teacher and the library media specialist should meet on a regular basis to discuss problems, results, etc. and amend plans. These meetings do not have to be long; notes will suffice in some instances.

10. The public library should be notified of topic(s) being researched by students.

THE COMPONENTS OF A DAILY LESSON

STATEMENT OF OBJECTIVE:

When the library media specialist and classroom teacher plan cooperatively they should determine the main objective of the lesson. It is recommended that the stated objective be visible to the students. It is important that the students know what they are expected to learn.

INTRODUCTORY ACTIVITY (warm-up):

Decide which professional is going to prepare the students for the library media center visit. This activity can be held in the classroom or the library media center. The "warm-up" can be simple or complex, depending upon the students and material to be presented. This introduction should supply the answer to "why" the students should perform the activity.

DEVELOPMENTAL ACTIVITIES:

At this time explain or demonstrate what the students should be able to do as a result of this lesson. Usually the library media specialist will direct this portion of the lesson. This activity can be held in the classroom or library media center, depending on the nature of the lesson.

PRACTICE ACTIVITY:

This is a sequence of activities the students perform which reinforce the skills introduced. These activities will generally be held in the library media center and it is most facilitative if the library media specialist and the language arts teacher "team" together and work with individual students who are having problems at this point.

INDEPENDENT ACTIVITY:

This portion of the lesson should mirror the "Practice Activity," without the immediate intervention of the library media specialist or language arts teacher, unless there is a strong need for it.

ASSESSMENT ACTIVITY:

The evaluation of the completed activities' success is determined by how well the objective was met.

CLOSURE:

It is important to conclude all library media center visits in some positive way.

PLAN FOR AN INTEGRATED OBJECTIVE
FOR NONFICTION AT THE NINTH GRADE LEVEL

Suggested Activities

The student may:

1. make a videotaped commercial illustrating examples of propaganda or methods of emotional appeal. The student must write the script before production.

2. listen to a tape or a record of a speech and identify facts and opinions.

3. write a speech of persuasion and record it.

4. conduct research on the background of the author of an essay or other nonfiction selection and write a paragraph or two on the author's qualifications to write the selection.

5. compare two articles on the same event taken from two different encyclopedias and write a paragraph or make a chart showing the similarities, differences, and accuracies.

6. use the *Readers' Guide to Periodical Literature* to locate magazine articles related to selections read in class and compile a bibliography of the references found.

7. compare the treatment of a current event in several of the major newspapers and write a one-page account of his/her findings. Some suggested newspapers are: *The Washington Post, Washington Times, Baltimore Sun,* etc.

8. conduct research on the life and philosophy of a current politician and write a campaign speech for him/her, or develop a whole campaign strategy—speech, slogans, poster, itinerary, etc.

9. use a variety of indexes to look for information on a controversial issue. After completing the search, the student will write a position paper on the issue. As an alternative activity, the topic can be investigated by a small group and shared with the class in the form of a debate or panel discussion.

10. conduct research on a local monument, historical building, or famous person in his/her own community or nearby areas—Bladensburg, Riverdale, Greenbelt, Bowie, Oxon Hill, etc. The student will need to consult the school library media specialist, the public library, and other community sources. Afterwards, the student will share his/her findings through videotape, slide/tape, exhibit, bulletin board or other approved method. Projects may be exhibited and/or preserved in the school library media center or area public library.

11. investigate the vocabulary associated with a particular career and collect a minimum of 30 words. The student will then complete a mini-dictionary of "specialized" words. For each word, the student should include the definition, syllabication, part of speech, and illustrations where appropriate.

*12. compile an annotated bibliography of resources in the school library media center on an assigned topic in nonfiction. (See sample form and student handouts.) Bibliographies may be filed in the library media center for future student reference.

*13. examine editorials in the newspaper on display in the school library media center and write a letter to the editor of a selected newspaper in reaction to one of its editorials. A student may earn extra points if he/she submits the letter to the newspaper and it is published.

*A detailed lesson plan is included.

Cooperative Planning Guide 1

STATEMENT OF OBJECTIVE (should be visible):

Using the card catalog and the *Readers' Guide to Periodical Literature,* the student will compile an annotated bibliography of sources on an assigned topic.

INTRODUCTORY ACTIVITY (warm-up):

location: classroom
director: language arts teacher

The student will copy these words and definitions:

Bibliography—A list of materials on a certain subject.
Annotation—A one or two sentence summary of the material.

DEVELOPMENTAL ACTIVITIES:

location: classroom
director: language arts teacher/library media specialist

The library media specialist reviews the information found on a catalog card and in the *Readers' Guide to Periodical Literature* and discusses bibliographic format. The library media specialist may highlight points in the discussion by writing them on the blackboard or an overhead transparency.

PRACTICE ACTIVITY:

location: classroom
director: library media specialist

The library media specialist distributes the student handout on bibliographic form and shows a transparency of a sample bibliography. Using the demonstrated format, the student will write an annotated bibliographic entry for his/her textbook.

INDEPENDENT ACTIVITY:

>location: library media center
>director: language arts teacher

Given a list of topics prepared by the library media specialist, the language arts teacher assigns a different topic to each student, taking care that only one student is assigned to a catalog card drawer in any one class. The students conduct their research.

ASSESSMENT ACTIVITY:

>location: library media center
>director: language arts teacher

The student will turn in to the language arts teacher an annotated bibliography of at least 10 sources on the assigned topic. The library media specialist may select the best ones to keep on file in the library media center.

MATERIALS/EQUIPMENT NEEDED:

>overhead projector
>
>transparency of sample bibliography
>
>blank transparency
>
>student handout on bibliographic form
>
>student handout explaining assignment

Note to library media specialist:

In discussion, stress that sources may be books, nonprint, magazine articles. Also, see the sample listing of topics with accompanying card catalog drawer number as a model for preparing a list to fit your library media center. The topics listed should be ones on which students can find a minimum of 10 sources.

Transparency of Sample Bibliography

Name_____

Bibliography of _____

_____,   _____,   _____
(Last name)   (First name)   (Title)

_____,   _____,   _____
(Title)   (Place)   (Publisher)

_____.
(Date)

_____,   _____,   _____
(Last name)   (First name)   (Title)

_____,   _____,   _____
(Title)   (Place)   (Publisher)

_____.
(Date)

_____,   _____,   _____
(Last name)   (First name)   (Title)

_____,   _____,   _____
(Title)   (Place)   (Publisher)

_____.
(Date)

Handout on Bibliographic Form

BIBLIOGRAPHIC FORM

BOOKS

Author—put last name first. Title (underlined). Place of Publication: Publisher, Date.

EXAMPLE:

Bach, Richard. Jonathan Livingston Seagull. New York: The Macmillan Company, 1971.

MEDIA SOURCES

Title of material used (in quotation marks), Kind of material—filmstrip, tape, etc. Title of the set if the material is part of a set (underlined). Name of producer, Date (if available).

EXAMPLE:

"Investigating birds," filmstrip. Birds. Coronet Instructional Media Company, 1974.

MAGAZINES

Author—last name first. Title of article (in quotation marks), Name of magazine (underlined). Volume number, Date (in parenthesis) pages.

EXAMPLE:

Lewis, D. "The New Navy," Aviation World. 69 (August 3, 1973) 33-41.

NEWSPAPER ARTICLES

Author—last name first. Title of article (in quotation marks), Name of newspaper (underlined). Section and page number, Date.

EXAMPLE

Smith, John. "Pollution in Prince George's County," The Washington Post. C5, January 4, 1981.

Handout on Topics for Bibliographies

TOPICS FOR BIBLIOGRAPHIES

	Topic	Approximate card catalog no.	Student assigned
1.	Adolescence	1	_____
2.	Adventure	1	_____
3.	Aeronautics	1	_____
4.	Africa	1	_____
5.	Airplane	2	_____
6.	Alaska	2	_____
7.	America–disc. and explor.	3	_____
8.	Anatomy	4	_____
9.	Animals	4	_____
10.	Animals–habits and behavior	4	_____
11.	Animals–stories	4	_____
12.	Archeology	5	_____
13.	Architecture	5	_____
14.	Art–American	6	_____
15.	Art–History	6	_____
16.	King Arthur	6	_____
17.	Arts and Crafts	6	_____
18.	Asia	6	_____
19.	Astrology	6	_____

20.	Astronautics	6	_____
21.	Astronomy	6	_____
22.	Athletes	7	_____
23.	Atomic Energy	7	_____
24.	Australia	7	_____
25.	Authors—American	7	_____
26.	Automobile racing	7	_____
27.	Automobiles	7	_____
28.	Baseball	8	_____
29.	Basketball	8	_____
30.	Birds	10	_____
31.	Blind	10	_____
32.	Botany	11	_____
33.	Canada	13	_____
34.	Careers	14	_____
35	Cats	14	_____
36.	Chemistry	15	_____
37.	China	16	_____
38.	Christmas	16	_____

Handout Explaining Assignment

ANNOTATED BIBLIOGRAPHY PROJECT

Due Dates:

_____ Receive assignment

_____ Turn in completed bibliography

Assignment:

Compile an annotated bibliography of at least 10 sources on an assigned topic. The bibliography must include at least one magazine citation. General encyclopedias such as *World Book* may *NOT* be used as one of the sources. Follow the bibliographic form discussed in class in writing the final copy and include a cover sheet.

Procedure:

1. Use indexes such as the following to find information about your topic:

    A. Card catalog, school and/or public library

    B. Film catalog

    C. *Readers' Guide to Periodical Literature*

    D. Other appropriate indexes

2. Make a list of all available material in bibliographic form. Suggestion: use 3 x 5 cards, one for each source.

3. Examine the materials available and make notes about the length of the article, pictures, charts, interest level, etc.

4. Alphabetize your resources and write your annotated bibliography in pen or type it.

5. Turn in your completed bibliography to your language arts teacher.

Cooperative Planning Guide 2

Teacher _____

Subject _____

Date/Time _____

# of Students _____

STATEMENT OF OBJECTIVE (should be visible):

Using newspapers in the library media center, the student will write a letter in reaction to an editorial or news article.

INTRODUCTORY ACTIVITY (warm-up):

location: classroom
director: language arts teacher

Given a set of statements, the student will identify facts and opinions.

DEVELOPMENTAL ACTIVITIES:

location: library media center
director: library media specialist

The student locates the section of the newspaper that has editorials and letters to the editor.

PRACTICE ACTIVITY:

location: library media center
director: library media specialist and language arts teacher

The student will find a letter to the editor that is a reaction to an editorial or news article in a current issue of that paper.

INDEPENDENT ACTIVITY:

location: classroom/library media center
director: language arts teacher

The student will write a letter to the editor of a newspaper in reaction to an editorial or news article in a current issue of that paper.

ASSESSMENT ACTIVITY:

> location: classroom/library media center
> director: language arts teacher

The language arts teacher will evaluate the letters the students write. Additional credit may be earned if the student submits his or her letter to the newspaper and it is actually published.

MATERIALS/EQUIPMENT NEEDED:

> Newspapers
>
> Set of statements for warm-up

PLAN FOR AN INTEGRATED OBJECTIVE FOR HISTORY OF LANGUAGE AT THE TWELFTH GRADE LEVEL

Suggested Activities

The student may:

1. investigate the history of the English dictionary and compare it to the dictionary today.

2. conduct research on the English custom of conferring titles.

3. create a dictionary of Shakespearean words. Library media specialist will instruct students in bookbinding.

4. make a list of foreign words that have been infused into the English language.

5. create a dictionary of modern slang. Library media specialist will instruct students in bookbinding.

6. make a list comparing British English to American English. For example: pram = baby carriage
   petrol = gasoline

7. identify the meaning of a list of acronyms through the use of *Acronyms, Initialisms, and Abbreviations Dictionary* (Gale Research Company) or other appropriate reference sources.

8. conduct research on the infusion of brand names into the English language. For example: kleenex, coke, and Midas.

9. create a map which illustrates regional dialects in the U.S. and Britain.

10. investigate the derivation of family surnames.

11. make a dictionary of the new words being infused into our language from computer technology and other fields.

12. compare the arrangement and content of abridged and unabridged dictionaries located in the library media center.

13. trace the development of the alphabet and include illustrations.

14. select an occupation that requires a specialized vocabulary and make a dictionary of words associated with that field.

15. make a list of the various languages spoken in the U.S. The student will include a map which identifies the location of these languages.
Examples: Spanish—Texas; German—Pennsylvania.

*16. videotape a debate on the question of bilingual education in the U.S.

17. create and videotape a morning talk show for the school.

*18. make a list of careers that require a good command of oral and/or written language.

19. compose a list of words derived from people's names, i.e., macadam, petri.

*A detailed lesson plan is included.

Cooperative Planning Guide 1

Teacher _____

Subject _____

Date/Time _____

# of Students_____

STATEMENT OF OBJECTIVE (should be visible):

Using library media center resources, students will conduct a videotaped debate on the issue of bilingual education.

PART ONE
RESEARCH

INTRODUCTORY ACTIVITY (warm-up):

location: classroom
director: language arts teacher

The language arts teacher will pose the following questions to the class:

1. What does it mean to be bilingual?
2. What problems face non-English speakers in the U.S.?
3. Should non-English speaking residents be forced to abandon their language? Why or why not?

DEVELOPMENTAL ACTIVITIES:

location: library media center
director: library media specialist

The library media specialist will review current sources of information for this topic (*Newsbank, Readers' Guide, Facts on File, The Great Contemporary Issues* series, SIRS, etc.). The library media specialist will describe successful search strategy (index to source) and generate a list of key words (see "starter list.")

PRACTICE ACTIVITY:

location: library media center
director: library media specialist

The library media specialist will locate the various sources mentioned above with students. The library media specialist will have a student look up one search word and explain why the information was or was not found.

INDEPENDENT ACTIVITY:

location: library media center
director: library media specialist

Students will continue search. This activity should take 2 to 3 days. (Schedule in plan book.)

ASSESSMENT ACTIVITY:

location: classroom
evaluator: language arts teacher

Students will have compiled information on bilingual education.

MATERIALS/EQUIPMENT NEEDED:

Bilingual key words starter list

Newsbank

Facts on File

Readers' Guide to Periodical Literature

Periodicals

Great Contemporary Issues

SIRS

Handout on Bilingual Key Word Starter List

BILINGUAL KEY WORD STARTER LIST

bilingualism

bilingual instruction

bilingual studies

education

curriculum and programs, elementary and secondary schools

intercultural education

aliens—education

ESOL (English Speakers of Other Languages)

PART TWO

VIDEOTAPE

INTRODUCTORY ACTIVITY (warm-up):

> location: classroom
> director: language arts teacher

Students will copy and define vocabulary. (See attached list.) Students will be divided into "talent" and "tech" groups.

DEVELOPMENTAL ACTIVITIES:

> location: library media center
> director: library media specialist

Day one:

Students will participate in a hands-on workshop on the use of the VCR and camera production techniques involved in producing a videotape.

PRACTICE ACTIVITY:

> location: library media center
> director: library media specialist

Day two:

The library media specialist will direct a practice session for the student. "Talent" group practices debate. "Tech" group practices using the equipment. Library media specialist aids students in working up their storyboard.

INDEPENDENT ACTIVITY:

> location: library media center/classroom
> director: library media specialist and language arts teacher

Language arts teacher gives final approval to research. Students conduct and videotape debate.

ASSESSMENT ACTIVITY:

> location: classroom
> director: language arts teacher and classmates

The videotape will be viewed by the teacher and fellow classmates.

MATERIALS/EQUIPMENT NEEDED:

  VCR equipment
  videocassette
  storyboard guide
  research notes

Handout on VCR Key Word List

VCR KEY WORD LIST*

audio

audio-dub

cue

dolly

fade

frame

input

monitor

output

pan

script

storyboard

videocassette tape

voice over

zoom-in

zoom-out

*Note: vocabulary from the list will be used in hands-on workshop.

Cooperative Planning Guide 2

Teacher_____

Subject _____

Date/Time_____

# of Students_____

STATEMENT OF OBJECTIVE (should be visible):

Using library media center resources, students will make a list of careers that require a good command of oral and/or written language.

INTRODUCTORY ACTIVITY (warm-up):

location: classroom
director: language arts teacher

The class will discuss the following questions:

1. Are there some occupations that require a better command of the English language than others?

2. What are some of these occupations? Student volunteer writes ideas on chalkboard.

DEVELOPMENTAL ACTIVITIES:

location: library media center
director: library media specialist

The library media specialist will describe career reference tools, their organization, location, and call numbers.

PRACTICE ACTIVITY:

location: library media center
director: library media specialist and language arts teacher

Students will locate materials and each look up one occupation mentioned during warm-up. Library media specialist will stop class at various points and point out cross references to related occupations. As a group, the students will decide whether occupations do need a good command of oral and/or written language.

INDEPENDENT ACTIVITY:

location: library media center
director: library media specialist

Students will continue research, language arts teacher will schedule a second visit if necessary.

ASSESSMENT ACTIVITY:

location: classroom
evaluator: language arts teacher

Students will have a list of occupations that require a good command of oral and/or written languages. Extra credit will be given for the most complete list(s).

MATERIALS/EQUIPMENT NEEDED:

Concise Handbook of Occupations. New York: J. G. Ferguson Publishing Co., 1976.

Dictionary of Occupational Titles. Third ed. U.S. Department of Labor, 1965.

Hopke, William E. The Encyclopedia of Careers and Vocational Guidance. Chicago, Illinois: J. G. Ferguson Publishing Co., 1977.

Occupational Outlook Handbook. 1980-81 ed. U.S. Department of Labor, 1980.

≡•≡•≡•≡•≡•≡•≡

Only two detailed lesson plans have been cited from a document that is one hundred and eight pages long. This kind of commitment to integration of library media skills into the English curriculum is an example of the leadership available at the district level even in these times of changing priorities in our educational systems. These lesson materials can be readily adapted for differences in collections and thrusts in curriculum, but cooperation by the library media specialist and the English teacher is the key ingredient. The delineation of tasks to be completed by each individual is clearly defined, but without communication, even plans as carefully developed as these from Prince George's County will fail.

7

School Level Integration
of Skills

Whatever technique is used at the system level to integrate library media skills and the English curriculum, the essential ingredient is communication between the library media specialist and the English teacher at the school level. The library media specialist must often make the first move and before making any gesture must be totally familiar with the goals and objectives of the course of study. In addition, the library media specialist must be willing to be flexible and to put in the necessary time to create a lesson that does indeed meet the specified objectives.

Very often at the senior high school level, the English teacher will approach the library media specialist to provide assistance to a class about to embark on a research project. This frequently occurs when the English teacher comes to the library media center to schedule the class for periods in which to do appropriate research. In actual practice, it is likely to be the classroom teacher who initiates the request for library media skills instruction in order to enable the students to successfully complete a given assignment. Then, it is the responsibility of the library media specialist to work with the teacher to provide a meaningful experience for the students.

SKILLS INTEGRATION IN
ANNE ARUNDEL COUNTY, MARYLAND

The example that follows is the result of the work of two library media specialists from Anne Arundel County, Maryland. They found that many English courses at the secondary level had listed objectives that required research in the library media center for the students to write a paper. In working with English teachers involved in these projects, the library media specialist was asked to present reference materials and books from the general collection to classes who were beginning to do research. A model was developed by a middle school library media specialist and adapted by a senior high school library media specialist who was working with the English teacher in an advanced composition class. The stated objective was: "the student will use at least five reference sources to develop and write a critical paper on selected works of one contemporary British or American author."[1]

Instead of presenting the selected reference tools herself, the library media specialist listed all of the materials that could be used by the students and had each student select a book or books, as appropriate. Since each student had a good idea about his or her subject of research, the materials selected had more relevance and meaning. After selecting materials, each student signed up to give an oral presentation of the resource(s) according to a specified format. The format was given in a handout, which guided the student in locating information and in preparing an oral presentation for the rest of the class. A reprint of the list of resources and the handout follow. The books on the list that are starred are included on the final examination; more will be said about that later. Each number listed under Special Reference Books represents a student assignment. The library media specialists who developed the list frequently include several titles for one assignment in an effort to cover the broad range of books available and to distribute the required work evenly among the students.

≡·≡·≡·≡·≡·≡·≡

SPECIAL REFERENCE BOOKS

Literature

DICTIONARIES, ENCYCLOPEDIAS, AND HANDBOOKS

1. *Barnhart, Clarence L., ed. *New Century Cyclopedia of Names.* 3 vols. New York: Appleton-Century-Crofts, 1954.

2. Barnhart, Clarence L., ed. *New Century Handbook of English Literature.* Rev. ed. New York: Appleton-Century-Crofts, 1967.

   Benet, William Rose, ed. *The Reader's Encyclopedia.* 2d ed. New York: Crowell, 1965.

   Gassner, John, and Quinn, Edward, eds. *The Reader's Encyclopedia of World Drama.* New York: Crowell, 1969.

3. Fleischmann, Wolfgang B., ed. *Encyclopedia of World Literature in the 20th Century.* 3 vols. New York: Ungar, 1967-1971. Supplement. vol. 4, 1975. Set is in process revision.

Reprinted, by permission, from Cindy Krimmelbein, library media specialist at Old Mill Middle School South, and Bonnie Thompson, then library media specialist at Broadneck Senior High School. Research Model for Advanced Composition, (Anne Arundel County, Md., 1982).

4. *Hart, James D., ed. *Oxford Companion to American Literature.* 4th ed. New York: Oxford, 1965.

    *Harvey, Sir Paul, ed. *Oxford Companion to English Literature.* 4th ed. New York: Oxford, 1967.

    *Hartnoll, Phyllis, ed. *Oxford Companion to the Theatre.* New York: Oxford, 1967.

BIOGRAPHICAL DICTIONARIES

5. **American Writers.* 8 vols. including supplements. New York: Scribner, 1974.

    **British Writers.* 7 vols. New York: Scribner, 1979.

6. **Contemporary Authors.* Detroit: Gale Research, 1962-date.

7. **Current Biography.* New York: H. W. Wilson, 1940-date. Published monthly and cumulated annually in a single alphabet under the title *Current Biography Yearbook.*

8. **Dictionary of American Biography.* 10 vols., index, and 7 supplements. New York: Scribner, 1927-1981.

9. *Dictionary of National Biography.* 21 vols. plus supplements. London: Oxford University Press, 1921- .

10. Kunitz, Stanley J., and Haycraft, Howard, eds. *American Authors: 1600-1900.* New York: H. W. Wilson, 1938.

11. Kunitz, Stanley J., and Haycraft, Howard, eds. *British Authors Before 1800.* New York: H. W. Wilson, 1952.

    Kunitz, Stanley J., and Haycraft, Howard, eds. *British Authors of the Nineteenth Century.* New York: H. W. Wilson, 1936.

12. *Kunitz, S. J., and Haycraft, Howard, eds. *Twentieth Century Authors.* New York: H. W. Wilson, 1942. *First Supplement,* 1955.

13. Magill, Frank N., ed. *Cyclopedia of World Authors.* 3 vols. rev. ed. Englewood Cliffs: Salem Press, 1974.

14. *The McGraw-Hill Encyclopedia of World Biography.* 12 vols. New York: McGraw-Hill, 1973.

15. Van Doren, Charles, ed. *Webster's American Biographies.* Springfield: Merriam, 1979.

    Webster's Biographical Dictionary. Springfield, Mass.: G. & C. Merriam Co., 1980.

16. Vinson, James, ed. *Contemporary Novelists.* 2d ed. New York: St. Martin's Press, 1976.

17. Wakeman, John, ed. *World Authors: 1950-1970.* New York: H. W. Wilson, 1975.

    World Authors: 1970-1975. New York: H. W. Wilson, 1980.

18. *Who Was Who in America: Historical Volume, 1607-1896.* Rev. ed. Chicago: Marquis, 1967.

    Who Was Who in America 1897-1981. 7 vols. Chicago: Marquis, 1942-1981.

CRITICISM

American Writers. 8 vols. including Supplements. New York: Scribner, 1974.
See full description of book listed under BIOGRAPHICAL DICTIONARIES.

British Writers. 4 vols. New York: Scribner, 1979.
See full description under BIOGRAPHICAL DICTIONARIES.

19. *Contemporary Literary Criticism.* Detroit: Gale Research Co., 1973-date.

20. Curley, Dorothy Nyren, ed. *A Library of Literary Criticism: Modern American Literature.* 4 vols. 4th ed. New York: Ungar, 1966. Supplement, 1976.

    Temple, Ruth Z., and Tucker, Martin, eds. *A Library of Literary Criticism: Modern British Literature.* 4 vols. New York: Ungar, 1966. Supplement, 1975.

21. Mainiero, Lina, ed. *American Women Writers*. 4 vols. New York: Ungar, 1979.

LITERATURE BOOKS FROM REGULAR COLLECTION

22. Brooks, Cleanth, Lewis, R. W. B., and Warren, Robert Penn, comps. *American Literature*. 2 vols. New York: St. Martins, 1973.

     Trent, William P. and others, eds. *The Cambridge History of American Literature*. New York: Macmillan, 1967.

     Bryer, Jackson, R., ed. *Sixteen Modern American Authors*. Durham, Duke University Press, 1974.

     Foster, Richard, ed. *Six American Novelists of the Nineteenth Century*. Minneapolis: University of Minnesota Press, 1964.

23. O'Connor, William Van, ed. *Seven Modern American Novelists*. Minneapolis: University of Minnesota Press, 1964.

     Weinberg, Helen. *The New Novel in America: The Kafkan Mode in Contemporary Fiction*. Ithaca: Cornell University Press, 1970.

     Stade, George, ed. *Six Contemporary British Novelists*. New York: Columbia University Press, 1976.

     Stade, George, ed. *Six Modern British Novelists*. New York: Columbia University Press, 1974.

24. Emanuel, James A., and Gross, Theodore L., eds. *Dark Symphony*. New York: Free Press, 1968.

     Gibson, Donald B., ed. *Five Black Writers*. New York: New York University Press, 1970.

25. Lewis, Allan. *The Contemporary Theatre*. rev. ed. New York: Crown, 1971.

     Nicoll, Allardyce. *World Drama*. rev. ed. New York: Barnes & Noble, 1976.

Handout for Oral Presentation on Reference Books

BROADNECK SENIOR HIGH SCHOOL
MEDIA CENTER

Directions: You will give an oral presentation of the literature reference book(s) selected by you. Please
examine your material carefully. You are required
to read the preface and introduction. Include the
following in your report:

1. Bibliographic information
2. Scope of book
3. Length of entry
4. Arrangement of book
5. Information included in the entry
6. Cross references
7. Photographs
8. Bibliographies
9. Index
10. Uses of or usefulness of

You may include handouts, transparencies, and
posters in your presentation.

The library media specialist checked with each student prior to the oral presentation to be certain that the student thoroughly understood the materials before the actual presentation. At the time of the students' oral reports, each class member was given a list of books to be discussed (the Special Reference Books list). The student list allowed space for note taking under each title. Special attention was given to the materials that were asterisked. Students were told they all would be responsible for questions on their final examination concerning these books. The students were also told that they would be tested on all of the books listed in the bibliography before they actually began their research. The library media specialist devised the test, administered it, and graded the results. Approximately three class periods were allotted to this activity.

The results of this planning and implementation were interesting. Although this class had been taught in the library media center in prior lessons, the students took the library media specialist seriously *as a teacher* for the first time. Several students had previously asked if one really had to go to college to be a library media specialist. They changed that attitude after this lesson. The library media specialist felt that the primary reason for this change in attitude was that she gave the class an assignment and she evaluated the results of that assignment.

The final examination included ten questions similar to the questions on the test over all the books in the bibliography. Since the students were required to use at least five sources in their papers and the results of the test were all above 75 percent, the consensus was that the lesson was a success. In addition to evaluating the tests, the library media specialist also skimmed the research papers, paying particular attention to the bibliographies, to further assess whether or not the students had selected the best tools for their specific topic. A copy of a test on special reference materials follows.

≡·≡·≡·≡·≡·≡·≡

TEST ON SPECIAL REFERENCE MATERIALS

Name_____   Advanced Composition

Date_____

TEST ON SPECIAL REFERENCE BOOKS: LITERATURE

Part 1. Multiple Choice (40 points)

Directions: Write the letter of the correct answer in the blank at the left of each question.

_____ 1. If you wanted a medium length entry on American authors during the 1700's, which would be the best biographical reference source to use?

   a. *Current Biography*

   b. *Webster's American Biographies*

   c. *American Authors, 1600-1900*

   d. *Contemporary Authors*

_____ 2. Which reference book contains entries on authors, plot summaries, character sketches, literary forms and outstanding works in world literature?

   a. *New Century Handbook of English Literature*

   b. *Contemporary Authors*

   c. *The Reader's Encyclopedia*

   d. *McGraw-Hill Encyclopedia of World Biography*

Reprinted, by permission, from Cindy Krimmelbein, library media specialist at Old Mill Middle School South, and Bonnie Thompson, then library media specialist at Broadneck Senior High School, Research Model for Advanced Composition, (Anne Arundel County, Md., 1982).

_____ 3. Which is the best source to consult for biographical information on world writers of this century?

   a. *Dictionary of American Biography*

   b. *American Women Writers*

   c. *Current Biography*

   d. *Twentieth-Century Authors*

_____ 4. Which reference source would you consult to locate brief information on authors, fictional characters, literary allusions, and literary works?

   a. *Contemporary Authors*

   b. *Oxford Companion to Literature* series

   c. *Dictionary of National Biography*

   d. *Webster's Biographical Dictionary*

_____ 5. If you wanted excerpts of major criticisms of the works of twentieth century poets, novelists, and playwrights, which would be the best reference source to use? This source includes living writers and those deceased since January 1, 1960.

   a. *American Writers*

   b. *A Library of Literary Criticism: Modern American Literature*

   c. *Contemporary Literary Criticism*

   d. *American Women Writers*

_____ 6. Which multi-volume biographical reference source would you consult to locate concise information on the life and accomplishments of deceased British notables? Bibliographies are included at the end of all articles in this source.

   a. *British Authors before 1800*

   b. *Dictionary of National Biography*

   c. *Oxford Companion to English Literature*

   d. *Encyclopedia of World Literature in the Twentieth Century*

_____ 7. Which reference book gives essential facts about proper names including persons, places, literary titles and characters, historical events, and mythological figures?

    a. *American Writers*

    b. *Dictionary of American Biography*

    c. *New Century Cyclopedia of Names*

    d. *McGraw-Hill Encyclopedia of World Biography*

_____ 8. Of the following sources which one covers the origin and development of masterpieces in American literature? Primary and secondary literature is included. The arrangement of the book is chronological. Social, political, and economic aspects of the time period are discussed as well as the various influences on the author.

    a. *Reader's Encyclopedia*

    b. *Oxford Companion to American Literature*

    c. *American Literature* by Brooks, Lewis, and Warren

    d. *The New Novel in America* by Weinberg

_____ 9. Which single volume reference source would you consult to find a biography, a bibliography, a listing of critical studies, and a signed essay on an important living novelist or short story writer in the English language?

    a. *Contemporary Novelists*

    b. *Twentieth-Century Authors*

    c. *Cyclopedia of World Authors*

    d. *Current Biography*

_____10. Which reference source gives extensive information on American authors? You can find biographical information, a critique of the author's works, and a lengthy bibliography at the end of each article.

    a. *Modern American Literature*

    b. *Dictionary of American Biography*

    c. *Who Was Who in America*

    d. *American Writers*

Part 11. <u>Fill in the Blank</u> (60 points)

Directions: For the following questions, list the best book source which would answer the question.

11. What is the name of the book on our list that includes essays covering aspects of style and thought of five black writers?

_____

12. Which reference source contains brief biographical sketches of prominent deceased Americans? The bare, minimal facts are given in abbreviated form.

_____

13. Which reference source would give you brief biographical information on world authors of the twentieth century and include a critique of the author's style and his works? This multi-volume work is in the process of revision.

_____

14. A list of books and articles on a particular subject is called a

_____

15. Which reference book is the best source to use to locate essential biographical information, comprehensive bibliographies, overview of writing style, and analysis of works of the best known women writers from colonial times to present?

_____

16. Name the reference source that covers basic biographical information on British authors prior to the nineteenth century?

_____

17. _____
    contains sketches of people of many nationalities prominent in
    the news. The sketches vary in length, often include a photo, and
    include references to other informational sources. This source
    was first published in 1940 and is published monthly with annual
    cumulations called Yearbooks.

18. Of the books listed in your bibliography, which book gives
    biographical and critical material on several American authors
    and their works? Each entry in the book averages about 50 pages.

    _____

19. Which multi-volume reference source is a bio-bibliographical
    guide to current writers in all media including journalism, drama,
    motion pictures, and television? These factual sketches include
    personal facts, career information, an extensive list of writings,
    work in progress, a Sidelights feature, and a list of biographical-
    critical sources for further research. Only basic facts are pre-
    sented. No evaluation of the writers works is given.

    _____

20. _____
    gives abbreviated biographical information on important persons
    of all nations and of all periods of time.

21. Which book on the list covers drama through genre? This book
    emphasizes the importance of drama in society.

    _____

22. Which reference source (4 volumes at the present time) would
    you consult to find critical comments on the writings of twen-
    tieth century British writers? Each entry contains bibliographies
    for all included authors.

    _____

23. Name the multi-volume reference source that gives detailed background information on people important in history including authors. This source is not limited to a particular time period. A portrait is usually included and there is a Further Reading List at the end of each article. There is a separate index in volume 12 of this set.

_____

24. If you wanted to locate biographical and critical information on a particular author in the regular book collection, how would you go about your search? Please be specific.

_____

_____

_____

_____

_____

_____

_____

_____

_____

Answer Key

Part I

1. C	2. C	3. D	4. B	5. C
6. D	7. C	8. C	9. A	10. D

Part II

11. *Five Black Writers*   12. *Webster's American Biographies*   13. *Encyclopedia of World Literature in the 20th Century*   14. bibliography   15. *American Women Writers*   16. *British Authors before 1800*   17. *Current Biography*   18. *Seven Modern American Novelists*   19. *Cyclopedia of World Authors*   20. *Webster's Biographical Dictionary*   21. *World Drama* 22. *A Library of Literary Criticism: Modern British Literature*   23. *McGraw-Hill Encyclopedia of World Biography*

☰·☰·☰·☰·☰·☰·☰

SKILLS INTEGRATION IN
MONTGOMERY COUNTY, MARYLAND

Gaithersburg Senior High School in Montgomery County, Maryland, has served as a model for senior high school library professionals throughout the state.[2] One of the primary reasons for this school's outstanding program is the involvement of the library media specialists in integrating library media skills with other facets of the school's curriculum, specifically the English curriculum. While integrating library media skills into the curriculum is encouraged and facilitated through the district's central office, it is the effort of the library media specialist at the school level that creates the atmosphere that allows integrated instruction to occur. The library media specialists at Gaithersburg know the curriculum; they have established good, working relationships with school administrators and teachers, and they know the level of students in the classes with which they work. Library media skills instruction is a high priority in the total school program.

Since the students at Gaithersburg use the library media center extensively for research projects, the collection includes some specialized resources. Among them are DIALOG and MICROCAT. DIALOG is a computer-assisted retrieval service. In addition to using the *Readers' Guide to Periodical Literature* to search for magazine articles, students can learn to search for articles using the microcomputer and DIALOG. This computerized database gives students access to information stored in bibliographic form in over one hundred files. As both the library media specialist and the student must be present during the search, the most convenient times for making an appointment to conduct a search are after school and during evening hours (Gaithersburg Senior High School's library media center is open two nights a week until 8 o'clock).

MICROCAT is a catalog on microfiche. All the high schools in Montgomery County are members of MILO, the Maryland Interlibrary Loan System. MICROCAT is a catalog on microfiche of materials owned by the Maryland public and university libraries who participate in MILO, including Johns Hopkins University and the University of Maryland. These materials may be borrowed by schools who belong to the interlibrary loan system, thereby opening up wide holdings to high school students. Among the specialized resources included in the Gaithersburg High School collection are also the *New York Times Microfiche Collections, Facts on File,* and *Social Issues Resources Series* (SIRS).

The library media specialists at Gaithersburg make certain that the visitors to their school understand that the work they have done in integrating library media skills with the English curriculum could not have been accomplished without the cooperation of the English teachers. As the senior high school has grades ten through twelve, the library media orientation begins with the incoming tenth grade classes. An overview of their schedule for the year as it pertains to English instruction follows.

≡·≡·≡·≡·≡·≡·≡

INSTRUCTIONAL PROGRAM OVERVIEW
1983-84

SEPTEMBER

Library Media Center Introduction for 10th grade Oral Communication and Narrative Literature Classes, one class period. (Slide/tape and tour of Library Media Center), 29 classes.

OCTOBER

Television Studio introduction for 10th grade Oral Communication classes, two class periods, 16 classes.

NOVEMBER-DECEMBER

Academic Research Techniques I (ART I) for 10th grade Oral Communication classes, four-day research skills unit, 9 classes.

Academic Research Techniques II (ART II) for 11th grade Language Writing Workshop classes, four-day research unit, 6 classes.

JANUARY

Assist students with semester research papers.

FEBRUARY

Television Studio introduction for 10th grade Oral Communication classes, two class periods.

MARCH-APRIL

Academic Research Techniques I (ART I) for 10th grade Oral Communication classes, four-day research skills unit.

Academic Research Techniques II (ART II) for 11th grade Language Writing Workshop classes, four-day research unit.

Reprinted, by permission, from Linda Crump, head library media specialist for Gaithersburg Senior High School, Virginia Lucey, library media specialist for Gaithersburg Senior High School, and Frances Dean, Director of Department of Instructional Resources, Montgomery County, Md.

MAY

Assist students with semester research papers.

SEPTEMBER-JUNE

Television Production I and CAMERA EYE—daily classes.

≡·≡·≡·≡·≡·≡·≡

A closer look at activities in the library media center as it involves tenth grade students is in order. Those activities that apply to tenth grade English include:

1. Library Media Center Introduction—a one class period session in September for every 10th grade English class (Oral Communication and Narrative Literature) featuring a slide/tape presentation and a tour of the Media Center.

2. Television Studio Introduction—two class periods for every 10th grade oral communication class highlighting the operation and production potential of the TV Studio. Students receive a brief explanation of equipment operation and acting skills. The session culminates with the students operating the studio equipment and acting to produce a one-minute videotaped skit.

3. Academic Research Techniques I (ART I)—a four class period research skills unit for every 10th grade oral communication class offering students a more in-depth involvement with reference tools and computer-assisted research (DIALOG). Academic Research Techniques I (ART I) is a part of a unit in an oral communications course of study entitled "Using the High School Media Center." The unit is organized to assist students with completing the research necessary to prepare for informative or persuasive speeches. The selection of topics varies depending upon the level of the individuals in the class. A model of the unit follows.

≡·≡·≡·≡·≡·≡·≡

UNIT ON USING THE HIGH SCHOOL MEDIA CENTER

Academic Research Techniques I

OBJECTIVES

Students will be able to:

1. Select appropriate sources of information for their research topic.

2. Use the *Readers' Guide to Periodical Literature* as an example of periodical indexes to locate specific articles.

3. Interpret an entry in the *Readers' Guide.*

4. Determine which magazines are available in the library media center and how to obtain them.

5. Differentiate between "hard copy" of the magazine and microfiche.

6. Understand computer assisted research capabilities as an index to periodical sources.

Prior to work done by the library media specialist, the English teacher will have discussed the speech assignment and due dates with the class. The students will have selected their topics before the library media specialist begins the Day 1 activities with the class.

ACTIVITIES

Day 1—Classroom

1. Where do you start to locate information in the Library Media Center?

2. View slide tape, "A Review of the *Readers' Guide to Periodical Literature.*"

Reprinted, by permission, from Linda Crump, head library media specialist for Gaithersburg Senior High School, Virginia Lucey, library media specialist for Gaithersburg Senior High School, and Frances Dean, Director of Department of Instructional Resources, Montgomery County, Md.

Day 1—Classroom (cont'd)

3. Practice reading several *Readers' Guide* entries (overhead transparencies).

4. Review procedure for checking out a magazine in the library media center.

5. Complete *Readers' Guide* review worksheet.

Day 2—Library Media Center

1. What is computer assisted research?

2. View slide tape, "Graffiti on a Database."

3. Divide the class into two groups. One group learns to use the computer and DIALOG while the other group begins to use the traditional resources to complete their individual research.

Day 3—Library Media Center

The two groups from the day before switch places—one group uses traditional resources; the other group begins to learn DIALOG.

Day 4—Library Media Center

Return graded *Readers' Guide* worksheet and answer any questions. Students continue research.

Handout on *Readers' Guide to Periodical Literature*

READERS' GUIDE TO PERIODICAL LITERATURE

DIRECTIONS: Complete the following questions. You will need to refer to the "Guide to Successful Use of the *Readers' Guide*," the paper entitled "Sample Entries from the *Readers' Guide*" and listing of abbreviations on the front pages of a *Readers' Guide.*

1. How does the *Readers' Guide* stay up-to-date?

    _____

    _____

    _____

2. Each *Readers' Guide* volume has the date printed on the outside cover. How do you think this information might be useful to you as you research the situation in Lebanon?

    _____

    _____

    _____

3. Where would you look to find out which of the periodicals indexed in the *Readers' Guide* are in our media center?

    _____

4. What do the abbreviations il, por, and SciDigest stand for?

    _____

    _____

    _____

5. Look under CONSUMER PROTECTION in the sample. What subject heading is after the SEE ALSO?

_____

6. Look under the subject heading, ASTRONAUTS. Using the 2nd article, list the following information:

   a. Name of the magazine

   _____

   b. Date of magazine

   _____

   c. Title of the article

   _____

   d. Author

   _____

   e. Page numbers of the article

   _____

7. Locate an article in the sample on each of the following topics. Record the name of the magazine, the date and the page numbers.

   a. Astronauts' space suits

   _____

   _____

   _____

   b. Television strike in the U.S.

   _____

   _____

   _____

c.   Speech by Kissinger

_____

_____

_____

d.   Verbal SAT scores

_____

_____

_____

e.   Banking with computers and without checks

_____

_____

_____

8.   Fill out the magazine request form as though you wanted
     to use the magazine in Question #6.

MAGAZINE REQUEST/SIGN OUT

Title of Magazine:

_____

Date of Magazine:_____

+ + + + + + + + + + + + + + + + + + + +

_____

Name of Borrower

_____

1st Period Teacher's Name

_____

Grade

_____

Date Due

Handout on Guide to Successful Use
of the *Readers' Guide*

GUIDE TO SUCCESSFUL USE OF THE
READERS' GUIDE TO PERIODICAL LITERATURE

A. *PURPOSE*

The *Readers' Guide to Periodical Literature* is a set of books which lists authors and subjects with magazine articles published by an author or about a subject. Not every magazine is indexed in the *Readers' Guide*. A list of the magazines indexed is given in the front of each volume.

B. *HOW THE GUIDE STAYS UP-TO-DATE*

Each bound volume of the *Readers' Guide* covers magazine articles published during one calendar year. The arrangement of the set of volumes is by year or in chronological order.

During the current year, paperback indexes are published every two weeks. At the end of the year, the accumulated paper indexes are put together in one bound volume.

C. *ARRANGEMENT*

Within each volume of the *Readers' Guide*, the arrangement is alphabetical. Authors and subjects are arranged in one alphabet. Under authors and subjects, titles are arranged also in alphabetical order by the first word, with the exception of The, A, and An.

Under a person's name, articles written *by* the person come before those *about* him. Subdivisions of a subject are arranged alphabetically under the subject.

D. *SYMBOLS AND ABBREVIATIONS*

At the front of each volume of the *Readers' Guide,* there are pages which list the abbreviations for magazines indexed and other abbreviations used.

E. *MAGAZINES IN THE GHS MEDIA CENTER*

The GHS library media center subscribes to most of the magazines indexed in the *Readers' Guide.* The list of these magazines as well as the issues we own from previous years is available on the index table.

Back issues of magazines in hard copy are stored in the periodical room. Many magazines older than 5 years are available on microfiche or microfilm stored in cabinets behind the circulation desk.

F. *INTERPRETING THE INFORMATION IN AN ENTRY*

Under the subject headings are the entries which contain specific information about the magazine articles on the subject.

SAMPLE ENTRY:

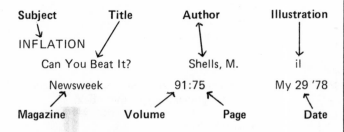

G. *REQUESTING A MAGAZINE*

To locate the exact issue of a magazine, you will need to follow these steps:

1. Find the article in the *Readers' Guide.* Check the "Periodical Holdings" list on the index table to make certain that the media center subscribes to the magazine. Is it on microfiche or hard copy?

2. Fill out a request form for each magazine. You will need:

    a. the name of the magazine

    b. the complete date of the magazine—month, day of month, and the year.

    c. the page on which the article begins. Many magazines have a limited table of contents. You'll waste time by not being able to turn directly to the exact page.

3. Ask a media center staff member to obtain the magazine (or microfiche) for you. The magazines are in the periodical room and the microfiche are in the cabinets located behind the circulation desk.

H. *CROSS REFERENCES*

Sometimes when you are looking for material on a particular subject, you do not find articles under that subject. Instead, you find a direction to look under another subject.

Video games. See Electronic Games.

At other times you may find a number of articles listed under a subject followed by a direction to look under additional subjects for more information.

Telescopes
 See also
Radio telescopes
Space vehicles—telescopes

I. *BOOK REVIEWS*

For reviews of individual books, see book review section following main body of the Index.

J. *MOTION PICTURES*

Motion pictures are indexed under the heading, Motion picture reviews—single works.

≡·≡·≡·≡·≡·≡·

Computer-assisted research is relatively new in comparison with the technologies of microforms, for example. However, such research is rapidly becoming a part of the library media specialist's expertise; specialists need to be familiar with the microcomputer as another resource in school library media centers. Montgomery County purchased DIALOG for all of its senior high schools, and library media specialists were instructed in its use. At Gaithersburg Senior High School, a student wishing to do a search via computer must fill out a form requesting the search (the form that follows) and work with the library media specialist until he or she is competent in doing the search. The student must be present for the search itself; the library media specialist does not do the work for the student.

≡·≡·≡·≡·≡·≡

Form Requesting A Computer Search

Gaithersburg High Media Center

REQUEST FOR COMPUTER ASSISTED RESEARCH

Student Name _____ Grade_____

Today's Date _____ Date Assignment is Due _____

Course Title and Teacher_____

Research Subject _____

Description of Subject _____

_____

_____

_____

Key words to be used in search (include synonyms, closely related phrases, scientific and technical terms)

_____

_____

Reprinted, by permission, from Linda Crump, head library media specialist for Gaithersburg Senior High School, Virginia Lucey, library media specialist for Gaithersburg Senior High School, and Frances Dean, Director of Department of Instructional Resources, Montgomery County, Md.

Database(s) to be Searched _____

SEARCH STRATEGY

_____

_____

_____

_____

_____

≡·≡·≡·≡·≡·≡·≡

Undoubtedly, there are many other examples that could be included in this book that could and do succeed for the library media specialist and the English teacher. These two programs have been observed firsthand by this writer and seem worthy of inclusion to illustrate the purpose of this book. It is important to remember that these examples could not have succeeded without the cooperation of both the library media specialist and the English department in planning, implementing, and assessing the projects. It is reasonable to expect that these examples will change with each school year as clientele changes and as curriculum thrusts change. The groundwork has been laid and the process is in place for continuing successful ventures.

NOTES

[1] Cindy Krimmelbein and Bonnie Thompson, Research Model for Advanced Composition (Anne Arundel County, Md., 1982).

[2] Gaithersburg Senior High School has twice received the Mae I. Graham Award given by the Maryland Educational Media Organization for exemplary library media programs in the state.

8

Shakespeare and Library Media Skills

REASONS FOR TEACHING SHAKESPEARE

What is taught and what is not taught in the realm of literature in the English curriculum frequently depends on the emphasis of the times. Certainly there are many works of literature from which to choose in order to satisfy a particular objective in an English course. Earlier in this book there was mention of the pendulum that swings back to the starting point if one is around long enough. This writer remembers taking a college course in the 1950s in Modern American Writers and being told by the college professor that F. Scott Fitzgerald was successful in his time but was in reality a "flash in the pan." English teachers did not use Fitzgerald, as a rule, when teaching American literature in the 1950s and 1960s. Today, Fitzgerald is back in vogue and his books appear in many curriculum documents; most secondary school library media centers have multiple copies of his works to satisfy the demand.

The one author who seems untouched by pendulum swings and who has probably been included as part of the English curriculum since its inception is William Shakespeare. If one were to take a look at the current *Books in Print,* one would see that there are a number of works with recent dates concerning the Bard of Avon. Shakespeare is not subject to elimination from an English course because of the emphasis of the times.

With this rationale, then, let us "brush up on our Shakespeare" in terms of library media skills integrated into the English program. In selecting Shakespeare to use as an example for integrating library media skills into the English curriculum, it is important to remember that many Shakespearean plays can be read in a senior high school. His plays can also be performed in high school. It is this writer's belief that every student should have the opportunity to be exposed to this great writer through whatever means possible. There was a time when only the college-bound student was permitted the privilege of enjoying Shakespeare's works—and too often, this is still the rule. The college-bound student will have further opportunities to expand his or her literary horizons; the student who will leave high school to go directly to the world of work may not have the opportunity again. Teachers and library media specialists must remember that in Shakespeare's day, the vast majority of his audience was illiterate. With the quantity of media available to present Shakespeare to high school students, there is little excuse for any student not to have access to this Elizabethan giant who speaks to us through the years.

If the English teacher chooses carefully which play(s) will be read, each student can find a play with which he or she can identify. One such play is *Romeo and Juliet*. Much that is relevant to today's adolescent is there—a love story culminating in a secret teenage marriage, families who do not get along with other families, intrigue and conspiracy on the part of a well-meaning friar, adults who do not understand their adolescent offspring, murder, suicide, and guilt. Teenage marriage, violence in our society, and suicide are all subjects that high school students frequently select when writing research papers. The spin-offs from this play are many and appear in a variety of art forms. The popularity of *West Side Story* speaks to the appeal that a modern version of *Romeo and Juliet* holds for adults as well as young people.

For the purposes of this book, then, *Romeo and Juliet* is the play that will be used for the high school English class. It does not matter, however, which play is selected. There are a number of areas where the library media specialist can take an active part in teaching integrated library media skills. In addition to exposing the students to the play selected, it is important that they have a grasp of Shakespeare, the man, and the time in which he lived and wrote. Students need to know about his Elizabethan contemporaries and the audiences that attended the Globe Theatre. This kind of information is usually prelude to the actual reading of the play. One sets the stage, so to speak. There are undoubtedly as many ways of approaching the study of Shakespeare's background as there are teachers of English. Whatever the method, the library media specialists should be a part of this endeavor.

What follows is one example of a way in which this important background information can be taught.

≡·≡·≡·≡·≡·≡·≡

LESSON PLAN FOR SHAKESPEAREAN STUDY

Background Information about Shakespeare

LIBRARY MEDIA SKILLS OBJECTIVES:

- Select print and nonprint materials for specific purposes.

- Extend skills in using all available reference materials.

- Select the most appropriate media form to communicate content.

PERFORMANCE OBJECTIVES:

- Given a list from which to select one topic, students in pre-assigned groups will locate at least three sources to use to do research on that topic.

- Given completed research on the selected topic, each group will present findings orally, using appropriate media, to the other groups.

TIME FRAME:

Five class periods.

TOPICS:

- The Globe Theatre

- Food in Shakespeare's day

- Shakespeare's audience

- Elizabeth I

- Life of Shakespeare

- Contemporary Elizabethan authors (Ben Johnson, Christopher Marlowe, etc.)

- The Black Plague

TOPICS (cont'd):

- Elizabethan fashions

- Costumes in Shakespeare's plays

- The players in Shakespeare's plays

- A day in the life of an Elizabethan family

RESOURCES:

- Card catalog, encyclopedias, indexes, bibliographies, vertical file, access to computer data base for search, audiovisual equipment and production materials (transparencies, cassettee and video tapes, pens, markers, paints)

ACTIVITY:

This activity is divided into two parts. Prior to scheduling the class to come to the library media center, the teacher introduces the project and divides the class into small groups. The groups decide which topic they will research.

Part 1.

The class comes to the library media center and spends the first day locating appropriate resources and writing an outline. On the second day each group will organize and compile the information for the chosen topic. Each group will decide what format it will use to present the information gathered to the other groups.

Part 2.

On the third and fourth days, the students will work in their groups completing the audio and/or visual portion of their projects. The final day provides time to review the finished product, practice the presentation, and to complete the written bibliography for their topic.

ASSESSMENT:

Each group will have located three sources on their selected topic and presented its findings using appropriate media to the other groups.

BIBLIOGRAPHY ON WILLIAM SHAKESPEARE
AND ROMEO AND JULIET

Print

Chute, Marchette. *Shakespeare of London.* New York: Dutton, 1950.

Frye, Roland M. *Shakespeare's Life and Times: A Pictorial Record.* Princeton, N.J.: Princeton University Press, 1967.

Garey, G. K. *Romeo and Juliet.* Lincoln, Neb.: Cliffs, 1979.

Goodwin, John. *A Short Guide to Shakespeare's Plays.* Exeter, N.H.: Heinemann, 1979.

Granville-Barker, Harley. *Prefaces to Shakespeare. Volume II.* Princeton, N.J.: Princeton University Press, 1973.

Harbage, Alfred Bennett. *Shakespeare's Audience.* New York: Columbia University Press, 1941.

Halliday, Frank Ernest. *Enjoyment of Shakespeare.* Westport, Conn.: Greenwood, 1978.

————. *Shakespeare and His Critics.* Cambridge, Mass.: Robert Bentley, 1952.

————. *Shakespeare and His World.* New York: Scribner, 1980.

Harrison, George B. *Introducing Shakespeare.* New York: Somerset Publishing Company, 1939.

Hazlett, William. *Characters of Shakespeare's Plays.* New York: Chelsea House, 1983.

Jorgens, Jack J. *Shakespeare on Film.* Bloomington, Ind.: Indiana University Press, 1977.

Lamb, Charles and Mary. *Tales from Shakespeare.* Totowa, N.J.: Biblio Distribution Centre, 1981.

Magill, Frank N., ed. *English Literature: Shakespeare.* Englewood Cliffs, N.J.: Salem Press, 1980.

May, Rubin. *Who's Who in Shakespeare.* (*Who's Who in Literature* series). New York: Taplinger, 1973.

Monarch Notes of Shakespeare's Romeo and Juliet. New York: Monarch Press.

Nolan, Edward F. *Barron's Simplified Approach to Shakespeare's Romeo and Juliet.* Woodbury, N.J.: Baron, 1967.

Parker, Barry M. *The Folger Shakespeare Filmography: A Directory of Feature Films Based on the Works of Shakespeare.* Cranburynswick, N.J.: Folger Books, 1979.

Quennell, Peter, and Hamish Johnson. *Who's Who in Shakespeare.* New York: Morrow, 1973.

Wise, John R. *Shakespeare: His Birthplace and Its Neighborhood.* Norwood, Pa.: Telegraph Books, 1983.

Nonprint

CHARTS AND POSTERS

Elizabethan Charts. Culver City, Calif.: Social Studies School Services. Includes 5 titles: *Elizabethan Seamen, Shakespeare's Theatre, Shakespeare's Kings, The Elizabethan Court,* and *Elizabeth the Queen,* n.d.

Voices of Destiny. Culver City, Calif.: Social Studies School Services. Full color posters: Includes Elizabeth I and Shakespeare. 16" x 22", n.d.

COMPUTER SOFTWARE

Black Death. Granville, Ohio: Strictly Software.
A simulation developed for the Apple II by Krell.

Romeo and Juliet. Larchmont, N.Y.: Media Basics, Inc.
Includes Apple II diskette with backup diskette, 16-page study guide, student resource sheets, and user's manual.

KITS

The Elizabethan Age. Mount Kisco, N.Y.: Guidance Associates, 1977.
2 filmstrips, 2 cassettes, and teacher's guide.

Multimedia Shakespeare. Bedford Hills, N.Y.: Educational Enrichment Materials.
Includes 8 filmstrips with cassettes, 24 slides, 3 posters, 1 paperback book—*Shakespeare for Everyone,* and a teacher's guide.

Shakespeare: A Day at the Globe. Mount Kisco, N.Y.: Guidance
Associates, 1977.
Includes 2 filmstrips, 2 cassettes, and teacher's guide.

Shakespeare Is Alive and Well in the Modern World. Mount Kisco, N.Y.:
Guidance Associates, 1975.
2 sound/slide parts and teacher's guide.

RECORDINGS

Ages of Man. New York: Caedmon, n.d.
Recordings from Shakespeare by Sir John Gielgud. Includes 2
12" LP records or 2 cassettes and paperback book.

Romeo and Juliet. New York: Caedmon, 1961.
Includes the entire script of the play read by Claire Bloom and
Albert Finney in the leading roles. Available in 3 12" LP records
or 3 cassettes.

Shakespeare: Soul of an Age. New York: Caedmon, n.d.
1 cassette contains excerpts from plays read by prominent actors
and actresses.

VIDEOCASSETTES

No Holds Bard: A Video Introduction to Shakespeare. Portland, Maine:
J. Weston Walch.
38-minute video production available in ½" Beta, ½" VHS, or
¾" U matic. For purchase or lease.

Romeo and Juliet. Mount Kisco, N.Y.: Center for the Humanities,
1979.
Production directed by Franco Zeffirelli and stars Olivia Hussey,
Michael York, and Leonard Whiting. 138 minutes, available in
½" Beta, ½" VHS, or ¾" U matic.

Romeo and Juliet. New York and Washington, D.C.: National Geo-
graphic Society, 1978.
36-minute video production available in ½" Beta, ½" VHS, or
¾" U matic. Also available in 36-mm film.

Romeo and Juliet. New York: BBC TV and Time-Life, 1979.
165-minute BBC production available in ½" Beta, ½"VHS, or
¾" U matic.

≡·≡·≡·≡·≡·≡·≡

ADJUSTING THE LEVELS FOR TEACHING SHAKESPEARE

Cliffs and Monarch briefs on *Romeo and Juliet* are included in the bibliography with no excuses tendered. Charles and Mary Lamb's *Tales from Shakespeare* would be a preferred source because they make such wonderful use of Shakespeare's language. Alas, it can be difficult to locate. As stated in the beginning of this chapter, this author believes that all students should be exposed to Shakespeare, inevitably there will be those who search out such helping resources as Monarch's *Notes*. But, as long as they have heard the words that Shakespeare wrote, what difference does it make if those students reach for a better understanding of the play?

In the lesson plan provided, the grade level does not necessarily matter, but the ability level does. The objectives could remain the same for all levels, but the teaching method would change with the ability level. As the plan is written, the library media specialist would provide help to each group according to need. With some groups of students, it might be necessary to spend that first day going through all the resources and helping each group locate the proper information. With other groups, the teacher may vary the number of resources required. If the group had a very low ability level, the library media specialist might work with the teacher to set up stations on selected topics and have the students go through the stations rather than have them do the actual reporting. There are enough commercial aids available to make that a relatively easy chore. The commercial media programs on Shakespeare could also be used, in part, for the student's final presentation to the other groups. The slide/tapes from the Center for the Humanities lend themselves to selective use. (The library media specialist must be certain that each slide is carefully labeled in order to assure that the slides are not misplaced and that complete sets are returned to their original carousel).

In working with slower groups, the library media specialist might suggest showing the entire videocassette of the play *Romeo and Juliet*—or the film if the proper equipment is not available for using the videocassette. Every student can be *exposed* to Shakespeare; every student will not necessarily have the ability to read Shakespeare and come away from the experience with understanding and appreciation.

It is important that the library media specialist understand the level of the class with whom he or she is going to work. It is equally important that the teacher and the library media specialist confer and understand exactly what the objectives are and what the library media specialist's role will be in the assignment. Is it necessary to pull the materials to be used into a reserve collection? Should each group be given a sheet that provides a research guide suggesting subject headings on a particular topic? Have the students had enough background work in research to pursue the task independently? If they have, one of the main functions of the library media specialist has been accomplished, i.e., making the student an independent user of libraries.

During the planning of this assignment, the library media specialist and the English teacher will want to discuss the list of topics to be researched by the students. Are there sufficient resources in the school library media center to adequately provide for each of the topics on the list? If it is noted that there are few available resources on the topic of costumes in Shakespeare's plays, for example, the library media specialist would need to locate materials elsewhere. The public library or the school district's central library might have sources that could be borrowed for the duration of the project. Materials would be located well in advance of the assignment to insure appropriate use. The bibliography included in this chapter is by no means inclusive, but it is representative of the kinds of materials that might be available through the library media center. The microcomputer could be used for a more inclusive bibliography giving the location of the materials listed to facilitate student access to resources outside of the school. A bibliography entered into the computer provides a current list of resources that can be kept updated as the need arises. The teacher, too, can quickly determine which media may be used with each class and each group assigned a specific topic.

Depending upon the level of the class with whom the library media specialist and the English teacher are working, there are a variety of ways to approach and culminate a research project. It is vital that the teacher and the library media specialist confer and understand exactly who is playing what role following clear delineation of the objectives.

When the time comes to complete the production aspect of the assignment, even the more adept students will require assistance. As the different groups decide how they will present their projects to the other groups, the library media specialist may establish stations that provide the necessary materials and equipment for specific kinds of production. For example, if a group decides it wants to make transparencies to illustrate the costumes used in Shakespeare's plays, a transparency making station would be set up that included transparency film, colored marking pens or pencils, a primary typewriter or rub-on letters, tape, frames, and an overhead projector with screen. It is a good idea to include sample student-made transparencies and simple directions to be followed to complete a set of transparencies, including overlays. The station approach to production allows the library media specialist and the teacher to move from group to group, assisting as necessary. The stations can be used over again for future classes. When the student production part of the assignment is complete and the projects are finalized, the library media specialist should be included in the assessment of the projects.

Being a part of the group research and production aspect of the assignment gives the library media specialist a good grasp of the student's entry and exit levels as well as a realistic awareness of available materials and center production capabilities. The contribution that the library media specialist can make in evaluating the final product is an important consideration.

The dual approach of using the talents of the English teacher and the library media specialist can give the student a true learning experience, one that includes a honing of library media skills, an appreciation and understanding of the work of one of the world's greatest authors, and a sense of genuine accomplishment. And the gratifying part of it all is that such cooperative ventures can be duplicated in a hundred ways for the benefit of the student.

9   *"Tomorrow and Tomorrow and Tomorrow ..."*

Throughout this book the problem of library media skills instruction at the senior high school level has been addressed. Indeed, concern for such instruction prompted the book. The reader must keep in mind that there is no *one* way to teach senior high school students successfully in library media skills or any other skills. By looking at a variety of examples where library media skills are integrated into the senior high school English program, one can see that there are a number of approaches; lesson plans appear in different formats and the methods vary greatly. One important interrelationship is obvious. The library media specialist and the English teacher must work cooperatively if there is to be a lasting impact on the student in the realm of library media skills instruction.

The reason it is important for library media skills to make a lasting impact on the student is that information and information retrieval will become increasingly important in everyone's future. Society has advanced beyond the point where any human being can know all the information necessary to survive in today's world. Estimates made about the quantity of information available in tomorrow's world are almost beyond belief. Students who are not taught how to locate information are being seriously shortchanged. If the process of integrating library media skills into the curriculum can help the student know what to ask for and how to locate what he or she is seeking, then the goals of the library media specialist and the teacher will have been met.

The library media specialist can begin the process of integrating skills one course at a time. Perhaps a realistic goal may be to attempt one course a semester and to work closely with one teacher until a set of lesson plans and activities is developed. Assess what is done along with the English teacher and make revisions as the project is implemented the next time. Gradually the library media specialist will have a collection of skills packages that can readily be adapted to all subject areas. Adaptations are required as course objectives change, as new technologies define strategies, and as library media collections alter. If skills for integrated instruction can be encouraged on a systemwide basis, each library media specialist can share what has been prepared in one school with other library media specialists in the system. Simple alterations are often all that is required to adapt someone else's plan to a specific need. Library media specialists who have used the integrated skills approach are knowledgeable about curriculum and can make valuable contributions when new curriculum is being written. These individuals find that they are such viable members of the total school program that they become consultants in a myriad of planning activities. This kind of involvement rarely occurs when skills are taught in isolation.

Those who benefit most are the students who will be graduating and who will be going on to other kinds of endeavors where retrieving information will be an important part of their world and where an appreciation for good media, whether it be in the form of literature or drama or television or film, will provide them with hours of constructive enjoyment. In this rapidly changing technological world where we live and work, having the ability to access information when it is needed will be the key to success, and being able to relax while reading a good book or while viewing a good film will be the key to that quiet place deep within where creativity is born. If this can be achieved, students will know that they were served well.

Appendix 1—
Materials for Senior High School
Library Media Skills

PRINT

Baker, Robert K. *Doing Library Research: An Introduction for Community College Students.* Boulder, Colo.: Westview, 1980.

Bee, Clifford. *Secondary Learning Centers.* Glenview, Ill.: Scott Foresman, 1980.

Bergman, Floyd L. *The English Teacher's Activities Handbook.* 2d ed. Boston: Allyn and Bacon, 1982.

Berman, Michelle, and Linda Shevitz. *I Can Make It on My Own: Functional Reading Ideas and Activities for Daily Survival.* Glenview, Ill.: Scott Foresman, 1978.

Bohlool, Janet. *Library Orientation: Syllabus.* 2d ed. Portland, Oreg.: National Book, 1975.

Brown, James W., and Richard B. Lewis, eds. *AV Instructional Technology Manual for Independent Study.* New York: McGraw-Hill, 1983.

Cleary, Florence Damon. *Discovering Books and Libraries: A Handbook for Students in the Middle and Upper Grades.* New York: H. W. Wilson, 1977.

Clendening, Corinne P. *Creating Programs for the Gifted: A Guide for Teachers, Librarians and Students.* New York: R. R. Bowker Co., 1980.

Cook, Margaret G. *The New Library Key.* New York: H. W. Wilson, 1975.

Hart, Thomas L., ed. *Instruction in School Media Center Use.* Chicago: American Library Association, 1978.

Jay, Hilda L. *Stimulating Student Search: Library Media/Classroom Teacher Techniques.* Hamden, Conn.: Library Professional Publications, 1983.

Karpisek, Marian E. *Making Self-Teaching Kits for Library Skills.* Chicago: American Library Association, 1983.

Katz, William. *Your Library: A Reference Guide.* 2d ed. New York: Holt, Rinehart and Winston, 1984.

Kemp, Jerrold E. *Planning and Producing Audio Visual Materials.* 3d ed. New York: Thomas Y. Crowell, 1975.

Kirkendall, Carolyn A., ed. *Teaching Library Use Competence: Bridging the Gap between High School and College.* Ann Arbor, Mich.: Pierian Press, 1982.

Laybourne, Kit, and Pauline Ciamciolo. *Doing the Media.* New York: Dantree Press, 1978.

Lolley, John, and Samuel J. Marino. *Your Library: What's in It for You.* New York: John Wiley and Sons, Inc., 1974.

Lubans, John, Jr. *Educating the Library User.* New York: R. R. Bowker Co., 1974.

Margrabe, Mary. *The Now Library Media Center: A Stations Approach and Teaching Kit from Kindergarten through High School.* Washington, D.C.: Acropolis, 1975.

Nordling, Jo Anne. *Dear Faculty: A Discovery Method Guidebook to the High School Library.* Westwood, Mass.: F. W. Faxon, 1976.

Peterson, Violet E. *Library Instruction Guide: Suggested Courses for Use by Librarians and Teachers in Junior and Senior High Schools.* 4th ed. Hamden, Conn.: Shoe String Press, 1974.

Rosenberg, Kenyon C. *Dictionary of Library and Educational Technology.* 2d ed. Littleton, Colo.: Libraries Unlimited, 1983.

Sears, Donald A. *Harbrace Guide to the Library and the Research Paper.* San Diego, Calif.: Harcourt Brace Jovanovich, 1973.

Shapiro, Lillian. *Fiction for Youth: A Recommended Guide to Books.* New York: Neal Schuman, 1981.

_____. *Teaching Yourself in Libraries: A Guide to the High School Media Center and Other Libraries.* New York: H. W. Wilson, 1978.

Thomas, James L. *Nonprint Production for Students, Teachers and Media Specialists: A Step by Step Guide.* Littleton, Colo.: Libraries Unlimited, 1982.

Thomas, James L. *Turning Kids On to Print Using Nonprint.* Littleton, Colo.: Libraries Unlimited, 1978.

Vandergrift, Kay E. *The Teaching Role of the School Media Specialist.* Chicago: American Library Association, 1979.

Vitale, Philip H. *Basic Tools of Research.* New York: Barron's, 1979.

Ziskind, Sylvia, and Agnes Ann Hede. *Reference Readiness: A Manual for Librarians and Students.* Hamden, Conn.: Shoe String Press, 1977.

NONPRINT

Computer Programs

Library Skills Package. Huntington, N.Y.: Right On Programs, 1983.
2 diskettes for Apple II, Apple II+ , or Apple IIe.

Using Reference and Outlining Skills. Baltimore, Md.: Hamden Publications, 1984.
2 diskettes, practice lessons, teacher's guide for Apple II, Apple II+, Apple IIe, TRS 80 III, or TRS 80 IV.

Kits

Camera Techniques: Single Lens Reflex Camera. Aspen, Colo.: Crystal Productions, 1981.
Sound filmstrip.

Developing and Printing—Black and White Darkroom Techniques. Aspen, Colo.: Crystal Productions, 1981.
Sound filmstrip or sound slide.

Developing Library Skills. Westminster, Md.: Random House, 1981.
6 color sound filmstrips (*Understanding the Library, Locating Books, Doing Research, Locating Facts, Using Periodicals, Using Nonprint and Equipment*), teacher's guide, 12 duplicating masters.

How to Survive in School: Using Library Resources and Reference Materials. Mount Kisco, N.Y.: Center for the Humanities, 1978.
6 sound filmstrips, sound/slide sets or videocassette.

Interpreting Visual Images: It Goes without Saying. Mount Kisco, N.Y.: Center for the Humanities, 1979.

Unit 1. *Learning to See and Understand: Developing Visual Literacy.*

Unit 2. *A Picture's Worth a Thousand Words: Interpreting Visual Information.*

2 sound/slide sets.

The Research Paper Made Easy: From Assignment to Completion. Mount Kisco, N.Y.: Center for the Humanities, 1978.
Sound filmstrips, sound/slide or videocassette.

Where to Go for What you Want: Special Problems in Library Research. Mount Kisco, N.Y.: Center for the Humanities, 1978.
Sound filmstrips, sound/slide or videocassette.

Word Processing on Your Microcomputer: From Keyboard to Print Out. Mount Kisco, N.Y.: Center for the Humanities, 1984.
6 sound filmstrips, sound/slide or video cassette.

Masters, Posters, and Transparencies

Activities for Learning: How to Use the Library. Portland, Maine: J. Weston Walch, 1975.
46 spirit masters and teacher's guide.

Building Research Skills. Portland, Maine: J. Weston Walch, 1980.
50 spirit masters or 50 copy masters for duplicating.

Dewey Dex Library Card Set. Logan, Iowa: Perfection Form Company, 1969.

Library Concepts Transparencies. Logan, Iowa: Perfection Form Company, 1973.

New Dewey Dex II Set. Logan, Iowa: Perfection Form Company, 1982.

Research Detective. Portland, Maine: J. Weston Walch, 1981.
26 spirit masters in 2 levels of difficulty, teacher's guide, and answer sheet.

The Research Project: Learning to Use Resources. Culver City, Calif.: Hayes School Publishing Company, 1982.
24 spirit masters—includes choosing a topic, examining sources, finding information in the library, and evaluating resources.

Appendix 2—
Associations for Library Media
and English Personnel

American Association of School Librarians (AASL)
50 E. Huron Street
Chicago, IL 60611

Publications: *School Library Media Quarterly,*
School Media Center,
Focus on Trends and Issues (monograph series)

Conventions and Meetings: Annual Convention with ALA,
Midwinter Meeting with ALA,
Biannual Convention

American Library Association (ALA)
50 E. Huron Street
Chicago, IL 60611

Publications: *Booklist,*
American Libraries,
Choice,
Books and pamphlets

Conventions and Meetings: Annual Convention,
Annual Midwinter Meeting

Association for Supervision and Curriculum Development (ASCD)
225 N. Washington Street
Alexandria, VA 22314

Publications: *Educational Leadership,*

Update,

Yearbook,

Booklets

Conventions and Meetings: Annual Convention

Association for Educational Communications and Technology (AECT)
1126 16th Street, N.W.
Washington, DC 20036

Publications: *Instructional Innovator,*

Educational Communications and Technology Journal,

Journal of Instructional Development,

Human Resources Directory

Conventions and Meetings: Annual Convention

National Council of Teachers of English (NCTE)
1111 Kenyon Road
Urbana, IL 61801

Publications: *College English,*

English Journal,

Language Arts Directory,

Books and pamphlets

Conventions and Meetings: Annual Convention